NOWHERE TO RUN

www.penguin.co.uk

NOWHERE TO RUN

The ~~serious~~ *ridiculous* life of a
semi- professional football club chairman

JONATHAN SAYER

bantam

TRANSWORLD PUBLISHERS
Penguin Random House, One Embassy Gardens,
8 Viaduct Gardens, London SW11 7BW
www.penguin.co.uk

Transworld is part of the Penguin Random House group of companies
whose addresses can be found at global.penguinrandomhouse.com

First published in Great Britain in 2023 by Bantam
an imprint of Transworld Publishers

A CIP catalogue record for this book
is available from the British Library.

ISBN 9781787636897

Typeset in 11.5/16.5pt Times NR MT by Jouve (UK), Milton Keynes.
Printed and bound in Great Britain by Clays Ltd, Elcograf S.p.A.

The authorized representative in the EEA is Penguin Random House Ireland,
Morrison Chambers, 32 Nassau Street, Dublin D02 YH68.

Penguin Random House is committed to a sustainable future
for our business, our readers and our planet. This book is made
from Forest Stewardship Council® certified paper.

*To my wife Lucy, thanks for all your help and coming
to watch lots of football even though you don't like it.*

*To Dad, thanks for the adventure so far! I hope
you don't hate this book too much.*

*To Jessie, my daughter. I hope you will like this book
when you can read and that you will enjoy football more
than your mum.*

To all at Ashton United, thanks for letting me into your world.

In memory of Keith Sayer.

*20 per cent of the author's proceeds will be donated
to Ashton United FC in perpetuity*

At any football club there's a holy trinity.
The players, the manager and the supporters.
Directors don't come into it. They are only
there to sign cheques.

– Bill Shankly

Contents

Author's Note

This book focuses on my first year as co-chairman and joint owner of Ashton United FC alongside my dad. While some of the events are recalled as they happened – or as faithfully as memory will allow – other details have been altered or exaggerated for comic effect and names changed to protect the identities of the many wonderful people who populate the world of non-league football. Other moments are in some way fictionalized, simply to make the reader laugh. Nothing within this book has been altered to protect Dad or me: all the stupidity and calamitous errors in judgement are real.

The Pre-match

We're 2–1 down away to Tadcaster Albion FC in our first round of the FA Cup. The first round of the pre-qualifiers, to be specific. It's beyond cold. The heavens have opened and I've learnt the hard way that there's a difference between a waterproof coat and a 'water-resistant' coat. Long story short, I am soaked and in a terrible mood.

So far it's been another bad day in the 'footballing office'. In fact the only thing vaguely resembling a positive is that my dog, Mabel, who's attending her first live football match, has been relatively well behaved.

There are twenty-three minutes left on the clock. The crowd of around 400 or so watch on, scattered unevenly like seeds about the Ings Lane Stadium underneath the greying after-noon sky. Myself and a group of about thirty-five away fans are huddled together, protected by the blue, rusty cover of the Ken Gilbertson Stand.

In the sparse breeze-block terraces a few yards away stand three old men wearing flat caps clutching pints of bitter in plastic pots. They seem totally indifferent to the rain pounding down on them. They are the Tadcaster ultras, the 'Taddy Boys', who for the majority of the match have mercilessly serenaded us with the number one song from their greatest hits.

'You're shit and you know you are, you're shit and you know you are . . .'

Dad is stood next to me wearing a puffa jacket so thick it easily doubles his width. He purses his lips, pretending not to hear, while I stare off into the middle distance, doing my best to look nonchalant (although I fear I just look constipated). Normally at this point we'd maybe take a walk around the ground together, but not today. After weeks of poor results and a building tension between us we've had an almighty row that's been on the cards for some time. It's all been a million times harder than either of us dreamed it would be and the experience has been demoralizing, time-consuming and financially ruinous. With both of us unwilling to apologize we are, at least for now, not on speaking terms.

Larry, a loyal supporter in his eighties, stares at me with lively green eyes that have no doubt seen it all before. His thin white hair blows loosely in the wind as he leans over to pass on his thoughts.

'The problem, you see, young Jonathan,' he says somewhat conspiratorially with a faint Welsh lilt, 'the three gentlemen singing, although tuneless, are quite accurate in their assertion. We are shit, and if you don't know it, I certainly do.'

I fold my arms uncomfortably and continue looking out into the distance, trying to appear calm and collected. I mutter something about 'staying positive' but the truth is I'm tongue-tied and lost. What's more, my new water-resistant jacket, as well as being incredibly unresistant to water, is also many sizes too big, especially in the arms, giving me the look of a child wearing a parent's winter coat. 'You're a fraud,' whispers the increasingly familiar voice in the back of my head. A sudden pang of insecurity rushes through me. I do my best to fight it, rolling my sleeves up in the hope that it will at least look like I'm wearing clothes that fit properly.

Little Mavis the tea lady, who always comes in her branded club apron regardless of the occasion (including a recent funeral not held at the club where she had no hand in the catering), grips on to her walking frame, her usually sweet face contorting in spite.

'Run harder, you bastards; you're not fit to wear the shirt!'

'Come on, Gran,' counsels Pete, her always jovial grandson. 'What did the doctor say about getting too worked up at the football?'

'And what did I say about being a patronizing little prick?' Mavis pecks back, instantly aware that she's more than won that round of the ongoing debate about her 'wellbeing'.

'This is bollocks,' asserts a bearded supporter behind us, a little too loudly for it not to be for my and Dad's benefit.

My fellow board members Angie and Robbo pace the terraces with pain-etched faces, while joint groundsmen Deano and Dale watch on like a pair of idle pall-bearers. They're all totally silent, unable to detach themselves from what's at stake if we lose.

'It's off field where the problem lies,' declares Frank Taunton, a curmudgeonly fan who has been against our tenure from the outset. 'What do they know about running a football club? The short-arse one's an actor and the big one doesn't have a clue.'

'It's like having Laurel and Hardy as chairmen,' agrees his equally misanthropic balding mate to a few laughs and ironic jeers.

Dad's lips purse even tighter in purposeful oblivion to the mini mutiny building around us as the clock runs down. His bombastic, never-say-die attitude has started to fade of late and for a moment I'm taken aback to see him look genuinely browbeaten. I'm still not big enough to apologize so instead clap my freezing hands together in a limp act of encouragement.

'You're shit and you know you are, you're shit and you know you are,' boom the Taddy Boys gleefully as our captain Jono Hunt gives away possession yet again.

'The question is,' Larry pipes up again, pausing slightly for dramatic effect (or to get his breath back), 'what are you going to do about it?'

Despite the Baltic cold my palms are somehow sweating.

'Well . . .' I begin unsurely.

'Who do you think you're kidding?' interjects the voice in my head, probing at my insecurities once more as I fiddle with my coat sleeves.

'I think that, er . . .' I muster unsurely, my voice warbling like a lark.

'Football is a tough world, young man,' asserts Larry. 'It's not for everyone. You might choose to take up a nice hobby instead. Pottery or birdwatching maybe.'

I feel the heat rising from my neck to my cheeks and begin to stutter a half-baked response about long-term projects and the building of Rome, but I'm thankfully put out of my misery by the sudden *thwack* of the ball being hoofed forward by our goalkeeper. A man simply nicknamed 'Tarantula'.

The ball flies up so far into the now dark sky that it should, by rights, come back down covered in snow, then – *thump!* – it bounces hard against the limey turf, bypassing the entire midfield. Tadcaster's until now reliable central defender goes to head the ball but mistimes his jump and collides into his teammate, allowing it to float over him and land right at the feet of our so far unprolific striker Boothy.

Time stands still and the crowd falls to a hush. Even the Taddy Boys briefly give it a rest.

Boothy looks absolutely terrified. He advances with trepidation on goal, visibly overwhelmed.

Suddenly, the suspenseful silence is interrupted by the tinny voice of Mavis. 'Hit it, you stupid sod!' she screams, her face curdling.

'Careful, Gran,' pleads Pete.

'Shoot!' implore the gaggle of away supporters.

'Please, please, please, please score,' I pray to myself. 'I will be a better person if we score. I'll give money to charity. I'll go to church on Sunday. I'll even build a church if this goes in!'

Boothy bears down on the 18-yard box. He picks his spot, shoots, but scuffs the ball horribly, practically rolling it towards the goal. Thankfully the opposition keeper over-commits. He dives just as the ball hits an almighty divot, squirming agonizingly underneath his body. It trickles over the goal line and nestles into the back of the net, sending the away fans into sheer ecstasy. We cheer, dance and celebrate as if we've won the World Cup. All is forgiven. Mavis embraces Pete, Pete grins, Old Larry looks up to the gods in thanks, and my dad's lips gently unpurse.

The FA Cup dream is still alive! The long road to Wembley remains intact! Not to mention the much-needed financial boost of winning a round of the FA Cup pre-qualifiers, the lifeblood of so many clubs at our level. I breathe the biggest, deepest sigh of relief in my life and, now slightly emboldened, unroll the sleeves of my new coat.

The flat-capped men are undeterred and for the remaining minutes of the match reprise their back catalogue, although now with slightly updated lyrics.

'You're still shit and you know you are, you're still shit and you know you are.'

'And they're still right,' says Larry, without missing a beat. 'It's going to be a long bugger of a season, young Jonathan. We were absolutely awful today. I could have played better, and that's saying something,' he adds, before gingerly picking up his walking stick and shuffling to the exit.

The final whistle blows and the agony is over – for a few days at least. It's not a good result but at least it's not another terrible one. The tie will be decided by a replay at our place on Tuesday.

The players trudge down the tunnel caked in mud and disappointment. Boothy leads the way, somehow looking more under the cosh than before he scored. Our fans do their best to applaud the team's efforts as the manager, Jamie Benshaw, storms down the touchline with a face like thunder.

'We got away with that – sorry,' he barks at Dad and me before disappearing from view.

We look at each other, unsure of whether we've just received an apology or a bollocking.

Tarantula runs around the pitch in some kind of misguided celebration. Perhaps he's miscounted the score, or perhaps to him this is genuinely as good as it gets. Who knows and, at this point, who cares?

Everyone starts to make their way to the clubhouse and Dad looks how I feel – overwhelmed by the journey ahead. I tap him on the shoulder and do my best to smile.

'Not too bad, hey Dad?' I mumble, slightly embarrassed.

Immediately he grabs me tightly and I'm suffocated in his dense puffa jacket.

'Let's not fall out about this stuff, son; we've got to stick together. I'm sorry I pissed you off.'

I unnestle myself from his arms and am totally taken aback to realize I'm crying.

'Love you, Dad,' I just about manage as I wipe my eyes with my stupid floppy sleeves.

For a moment there's a sense of resolve between us, not of jubilation but rather a creeping sense of optimism that this might be the fun adventure we hoped it would be a few months ago. A chance to achieve something together and also to become closer to each other.

We stay standing for a while as the crowd disperses. For the first time in weeks I can feel some of the anxiety I've been carrying melt away into the night sky with the condensation of my breath. Away from the ever-watchful gaze of Larry, the rancour of Frank Taunton and the incessant crowing of the Taddy Boys, I'm able to see the possibility of a distant horizon for the first time in a while.

There's near stillness in the now empty Ken Gilbertson

Stand. With only the hum of the electric floodlights and the distant sound of post-match debate coming from the club-house, I close my eyes and have a moment of actual calm.

It's short-lived though. My bubble of new-found serenity is burst by a bemused-looking man in Tadcaster overalls and heavy-rimmed bifocals.

'Hey, pal,' he says gruffly, poking me on the shoulder, 'is that your dog on the pitch? Because it's shitting on the half-way line.'

I nod solemnly, roll up my sleeves and make my way over to the halfway line. Dad heads to the car to prep for the three-hour drive home.

'You're ridiculous,' observes the voice in the back of my head as I plod across the battered turf, poo bag in hand.

'Maybe it would be fun to learn how to use a kiln,' I think to myself.

The following is a story about foolish optimism, giving your all and often coming up short. Regrettably it's mostly about losing, but very occasionally it's also about winning.

It's about a father and son from very different worlds who find themselves joined by the very same ambition: to save their local football club and, in doing so, perhaps their relationship too.

This is a book all about my love of a side of the beautiful game unseen by TV cameras, *Match of the Day* and Sky Sports. This is the wonderful and slightly crazy world of non-league football, and what follows is the (partly) true story of my and Dad's first season as co-chairmen and owners of Ashton United FC.

Part One

Part One

1

Mind the Gap

We walk through the car park of Lionel's Lino Emporium with a spring in our step and smiles on our faces. The sun shines down optimistically on the granite trading estate as Dad and I, dressed in our Sunday best, approach the converted mill. A banner pasted to the brickwork of the building proudly declares it to be 'The home of the greatest collection of high-quality lino and flooring solutions in the Greater Manchester area'.

I press the buzzer on the steel-clad door and wait for a response. We're here for our morning meeting with Tony Liverstout, son of the late Lionel Liverstout, and now sole owner and proprietor of the emporium.

A sense of nervous excitement rushes through my body. Today is, after all, a very big day. After several months of discussions, plenty of back and forth via email and increasingly regular meetings, we're about to officially become the new joint chairmen and co-owners of Ashton United, a semi-professional football club based in Ashton-under-Lyne plying its trade in the seventh tier of English football, 158 places

below the top of the Premier League. I can hardly suppress
my glee!

For anyone reading this who detects a note of sarcasm,
you're totally wrong. For me this is a genuinely thrilling prospect. It's an opportunity to step out of my comfort zone and
propel myself head first into a world I have long been madly
in love with. The world of sport. A world that, as someone
who makes their living in theatre and is anything but athletic,
has been very much closed to me until this point. In fact this
very moment, waiting outside Tony's inherited floor solution
empire, represents the realization of a pipe dream I've had
since I was eight years old, when I first watched the team play.
A cold midweek night twenty-five years ago, when the mighty
Robins were defeated 3–1 by Ossett Albion in the Unibond
Northern Premier League.

I can still remember attending that game, my first ever live
football match, with vivid clarity, and recollect the sense of
awe and wonderment that came with it. The clink and clank of
the rusty turnstile rolling us in, our bodies jostling up against
the crowd before settling on the concrete terraces to watch the
match. Being presented with a match-day programme and a
red and white scarf by Dad. I can still smell the meat and
potato pies mingling with Bovril in the Tuesday-night air,
and hear the shrill sound of the ref's whistle as we kicked off. I
can recall the condensation rising from the grass, illuminated
under the atmospheric, slightly flickering floodlights at the
Hurst Cross Stadium. The thrill of hearing the players and
managers up close and unfiltered. The intoxicating feeling of
being surrounded by adults shouting and swearing at the referee, despite my company.

It was a spellbinding experience, one where I first felt part of something bigger than myself. I stood on the terrace at just under four feet, wearing a large red bobble hat twice the size of my head, aware that I was undergoing some kind of rite of passage. Stepping out of childhood and hovering tantalizingly on the precipice of manhood.

Football has always been a huge part of our family. As a fairly repressed and secular bunch it's been both our therapy and our church. The source of jubilation and despair, and the cause of many a bitter argument. To nick from, and badly paraphrase, the great Bill Shankly, 'Some say football is a matter of life and death, but they're wrong. It's much more important than that!'

I've always regarded the sport as a worthy spanner in the toolbox of social survival. No matter the place, no matter the company, it's allowed me to find common ground. From Manchester to Manhattan, Blackburn to Bali, I've been able to make friends through football. The most tense and awkward of meetings have been lubricated by the simple question 'Did you see the game last night?' It's a technique that's so often carried me through school, college and into adult life.

I come from a long line of large, broad, red-headed men who've all had some success within the lower echelons of the game. My great-grandad played for Accrington Stanley. My grandad, Johnny Burke, was a local hero, making more appearances for Ashton United than any other player in our history. He also captained the side during our only ever serious FA Cup run back in 1952 and was part of setting up local rivals Curzon after that. My dad, although not as technically gifted (but equally large and ginger), played a few years for

Curzon and later AFC Hillgate. He also managed to write himself into the local history books, albeit for most sendings-off and bookings in a single season. One of which was for punching a left-half who 'asked your mum out' mid-match.

I certainly did not inherit any footballing ability. I'm five foot six and a half, incredibly skinny with wiry dark hair, asthma and a squeaky voice, meaning I sound and look like I'm yet to cross that precipice I stood at all those years ago (namely, manhood). To this day I am full of a quiet self-loathing about my inability to do more than five keepy-uppies. In fact being asked to do this in front of people remains one of my biggest personal fears after a scarring summer school experience.

As a youngster, I was not only habitually picked last in PE, but sometimes not even picked at all. I would simply drift about the playground while others enjoyed themselves, watching on longingly. I played my only competitive game for AFC Stanley Tigers under-13s in the mid-to-late nineties where I was brought on as a half-time replacement and suffered the ignominy of being substituted shortly after that. During my brief debut I managed to be at fault for four opposition goals, snatching a 3–4 defeat from the jaws of certain victory. After this match Accrington Stanley FC ended its affiliation with the Tigers, although I comfort myself safe in the knowledge that this must have been a coincidence.

The last football match I played in was for charity. In the Polish city of Kraków, a ragtag bunch of performers took on a team of low-level ex-professionals and local civil servants (how this match came to be is another book in and of itself). My main contribution was to run the length of the pitch only to blaze my shot well over the bar and vomit on the sidelines after over-exerting myself.

The sad truth is, the only things I've inherited with regard to football are my passion and enthusiasm. I always accepted my participation as being restricted to that of an unrequited lover – always there but never needed. Following the team home and away, at all costs. Devoted and unnoticed. Or worse, noticed but unwanted. I spent my teenage years reading and memorizing Opta stats and figures, building up a semi-professional player database in my head that could rival the most experienced and well-travelled ground hopper. I would rarely miss a match at Hurst Cross.

Once the time finally came for me to fly the nest and leave home, no matter where I found myself I always followed the club's fortunes from afar. Whether things were on the up or (as was often the case) on the way down. Wherever in the world work has taken me I've always taken the (now battered) match-day programme from that game against Ossett Albion. I was forever itching to find a way to feel connected to my boyhood club despite my now living in London. So it stood to reason that when I arrived back at my flat one night (over four years ago now) and saw an SOS tweet flash up from the club's official Twitter account seeking urgent help and involvement, I couldn't help but feel it was a message. Well, it was obviously a message, but I mean something deeper. It felt like a steer from the universe calling me home to the town I grew up in to be reunited with my first love. Only this time my feelings of devotion might be reciprocated. It was an opportunity to do something useful for the community and potentially re-find myself after a period of feeling increasingly untethered in the Big Smoke.

Finally, Tony greets us at the door. He's dressed in grey trousers and a white shirt. He has a hard, pale face and a thin tuft of brown hair.

'Sorry for the delay, gents. Men's problems. You know how it is,' he states bluntly before leading the way upstairs.

I follow, not knowing 'how it is' and hoping I never will.

We're led across an open-plan office with pinkish cream walls and IKEA-style pine furniture. The place is strewn with an impressive array of flooring test samples. PVC, rubber, tile, carpet and even the odd piece of AstroTurf are liberally scattered across the premises. As we go on I spot a poster pinned to a cork board on the wall. In it, Tony is wearing a stetson and boots. Below him is a message that reads WALK THE LINO – ARRIVE TO WORK ON TIME. I get the feeling he's walked us past it on purpose as he immediately notices the second it's caught my eye.

'I made a few of them,' he chuckles. 'We're never too busy to have fun here,' he adds as we walk past.

Judging by the looks on everyone's faces, Tony is right. They're not too busy at all, but I wouldn't say there's an abundance of fun going on either. The office feels slightly aimless, staff milling about making instant coffee, staring at their computer screens and shaking off hangovers.

'Which knob's nabbed my stapler?' someone shouts as we're led round the corner and bundled into the meeting room. It's a simple space with a faux-mahogany rectangular table, black chairs and a glass wall that allows you to see out into the main working space. Like a squash court, but with people talking balls rather than hitting them.

'Let's get down to business then,' Tony announces, taking

out a worn blue folder containing several recently printed documents bearing the official club and FA logos. I feel a flutter of anticipation in my stomach as Dad rubs his hands together.

'Here we go!' he says, retrieving a silver pen from the front of his checked shirt.

'I just want to say again how pleased we all are that you're doing this,' Tony adds. 'I'll admit after fifteen years I've taken the place as far as I can. Like a savings account after Christmas, I'm spent.'

He pauses, I think to allow for laughter, which I duly and nervously provide. He appears surprised. I fall silent and look down at the table.

'We need new ideas, young blood,' Tony continues earnestly.

I go to respond but my sixty-five-year-old father has taken the mention of 'young blood' as his cue and bursts into a monologue that, over the last month, has become more than familiar to me.

'I'm a businessman,' he explains, rubbing his fingers across his stubbled face. 'So I'll run the club as a business. Not spending what we don't have and keeping my eyes on the income. That's how I've always run my business, like a business.'

Tony seems impressed by this, and not at all troubled by my dad's use of simile, likening a business to a business. 'Shrewd,' he remarks, nodding like a dog (now *that's* a simile).

'Yeah,' agrees Dad, mirroring Tony's body language.

I feel a pang of irritation. Maybe it's concern about looking like the junior partner in the room or from watching Dad agree with himself so unironically, but I feel a sudden need to make my presence felt in the meeting.

'I have many ideas for the club,' I add, using a voice much deeper than my own.

Dad throws a concerned glance in my direction. I have no idea why I've changed my voice. It just came out, and now, caught in no-man's-land, I'm unable to retreat. I have no option but to continue.

'Like what?' asks Tony, his tone slightly harsher.

I feel my throat constrict and my mouth dry. I swallow hard and try to speak.

'There's loads,' I reply unsurely in a deep bass.

Everyone, including me, looks momentarily bemused. I feel a pang of shame and vow to myself to do better. I also decide to stealthily slide my voice back to its natural timbre as the meeting continues.

'Shall we crack on?' muscles in Dad, holding up his silver pen once again.

Tony suddenly leans forward, sporting a serious expression. He checks the room quickly to convince himself there's no one else in earshot. 'There was one thing I wanted to mention,' he says in the hushed tone of a man about to empty his soul in a confessional. 'So it's not a nasty little surprise when you find it.'

I have no idea what he's talking about and edge forward on my chair, moving closer to Tony and his imminent revelation.

'I told you there's no debt at the club, which is true, except there's a small gap in the funding that I've always covered from my own pocket. I don't want anyone to know though, if that's all right.'

'How much?' I ask, my voice still trapped in its foreign Barry White-esque register.

'Not much. It's for the coaches to the away games,' Tony

replies. 'They cost about £700 give or take, so we don't need it when we're at home.'

'So it's a shortfall of about £350 a week?' I confirm, sneakily sliding my voice up a semitone.

'Aye, thereabouts,' Tony fires back.

We reassure Tony that this won't be an issue. We can cover the gap between us until we find a sponsor, and his secret is safe.

'Thanks,' he replies, before remarking, 'We did used to have a sponsor. A local deckchair company, but they folded.'

Tony's face is so remarkably deadpan that again I'm not sure if this is a joke. Given that the nearest beach is 50 miles away I decide it's safest to assume humour and laugh. Tony looks affronted.

'He was a good friend of mine,' he says. 'Put his everything into that company.'

Dad chucks another glance my way and we sit in an unpleasant silence.

I look around, trying to distract myself, and spot another poster on the wall next to the glass partition. In this one Tony is dressed as an old-school mafia boss with a cigar in his mouth. The text below reads LINO SMOKING INDOORS. Tony spots me looking and smiles slightly out of one side of his mouth. I wonder if he's messing with me.

'Did anyone see the match last night?' I venture, without any particular match in mind, again subtly modifying my voice. It's the right thing to say, and the conversation gets back on track. Tony remarks that the red card was 'unbelievable' while Dad waxes lyrical about the quality of the finishing throughout. I don't know which match we're talking about but find myself agreeing enthusiastically.

Tony takes this moment of re-established social ease to return to the contracts and gently pushes the blue folder towards us. 'Let's get this done,' he says with confidence. We take the silver pen, and just like that it's signed, sealed and delivered. Dad first, then me. We're now joint chairs and owners of Northern Premier League side Ashton United FC. A new era at the club has begun and the ventilated office air feels full of possibility.

Angie, Tony's accountant and the club treasurer, bursts in right on cue, carrying a tray of mugs of milky tea. She's a kindly faced woman with an infectious smile and tight dark bobbed hair.

'Didn't have anything fizzy but thought it might be nice to raise something to the future,' she sings.

We make a few toasts with our builders' brews and find ourselves exchanging more pleasantries. Angie lets us know she is going to be working 'flexi-time' so she can help look after her new granddaughter. Apparently June is a bad time for the flooring solution business. Tony declares that owning a timeshare is one of the only sensible things you can do nowadays. I don't ask why, and pretty shortly after that we're done. We all shake hands warmly and retrieve our coats and bags, ready to head off.

'Any final advice?' I hear myself asking, my voice reassuringly back to normal.

'Try to enjoy it,' Tony replies flatly, blowing out his cheeks. 'It's like a rollercoaster at Blackpool. Plenty of ups and downs, not always well attended, and occasionally someone dies.' I again have no idea if this is a joke.

There's no time to find out though as on those words of

encouragement he grabs the contracts and leaves. As he does so, I notice an odd expression on his face that I can't quite place. Maybe it's men's problems? I don't dwell on it and we start to make a move ourselves, gathering up our copies of the paperwork.

Angie hangs back for a moment, watching Tony through the glass as he bombs down the corridor past the sea of discarded lino cuttings and into the privacy of his office. She turns back and smiles, but she's uneasy somehow, like she's weighing something up.

'Everything all right, Ange?' I ask gently.

'Absolutely smashing, chuck!' she bats back, a little too enthusiastically.

'Are you sure?' Dad presses.

She pauses for a moment, fiddling nervously with the lapels of her purple jacket, looking more than a little flushed.

'Well . . . there is a little something,' she whispers.

Dad unzips his coat and we slide back into our office chairs with a bump. Angie looks really worried now, like she's pushing herself to find the courage to spill whatever beans she's carrying. For a brief moment I see a look of concern flash across Dad's face.

'You see, I've always done the books for Tony,' Angie begins, anxiously flicking her neat brown bob behind her ears. 'He's got a lot of skills but not when it comes to figures.'

'How do you mean?' I enquire, doing my best to appear open and personable.

She double-checks through the glass again, peering out on the wider office population, before continuing to unburden herself.

'Well, non-league wages change all the time. Some of the players are on contracts but some are pay as you play. Last year our squad was a bit of a revolving door, with different lads playing each week, so the manager would agree a fixed fee each time.'

'I see,' Dad says in a tone that suggests he doesn't actually see.

'Last season some of the better lads wanted to leave, so Jamie had to increase their money and put a couple on contract, pay a few one-off fees, and it just sort of snowballed.'

Angie looks quite emotional. It's clear she's been carrying this for some time. She's taking shorter breaths and her speech is speeding up like a barrel of words rolling down a hill, getting faster and faster with every sentence.

'Basically it means the numbers Tony had didn't actually match up with the numbers we were paying. We did the contracts without telling him and then settled the one-off fees after the match when he wasn't looking. The extra money doesn't show up on the bank statements.'

'Shit,' I say, my voice now sliding up beyond its natural register as I slowly start to catch up with what is being said. 'And where does the extra money come from, Ange?'

Angie looks at her feet for a moment, almost like a naughty schoolchild.

'My bank account,' she says solemnly. 'We've not done anything wrong, I just didn't want Tony to worry, but it does mean there's a bit of a . . .'

'Gap?' Dad asks morosely.

'Exactly,' Angie confirms. 'Tony still doesn't know, but I thought you should. I just really wanted us to stay up and I had a bit of money from when Mum passed.'

Angie looks pretty defeated. She mops her tears away with a hanky and we fall into silence. After a few moments have passed I ask her roughly how big the gap might be.

'It depended on the week but I'd say it's about £400 give or take.'

'Jesus,' Dad says, the weight of the news slapping him across the face like a wet fish. 'We've already said we'll increase the wages by a grand a week. Plus the coaches.'

'When did we agree that?' I ask alarmed, my voice sneaking up another semitone.

'We'll talk about it later,' he reassures me. 'I didn't think you'd mind.'

'Coaches?' asks Angie before I can offer any response.

'Tony pays for the coaches on the quiet,' replies Dad, immediately outing Tony. 'Shit, sorry, not supposed to say that,' he adds.

I hastily reach for the discarded silver pen and jot down some numbers on the bottom of my copy of the contract. I can feel a rising sense of panic burning at my ears.

'Forty-two weeks in a season. So that's £350, plus £400, plus the extra grand you've agreed on the wages, times forty-two. That's seventy-three and a half grand we don't have,' I say aloud to nobody in particular.

'Is the grand gross or net?' Angie enquires.

'How do you mean?' replies Dad, a little sharply.

'You've got to add PAYE and National Insurance, so it's more like £1,200,' says Angie, having regained her composure after sharing and halving her problem.

I can feel a bowling-ball-like weight in my stomach. I start bashing numbers into a calculator in the hope of getting a different answer from the one in my head.

'It's a deficit of near £82K a year,' I conclude soberly.

'Plus the overdue invoices,' adds Angie unhelpfully, tightening the screw even more.

Dad looks on, his face now fully flushed and perspiring.

'Has Tony not mentioned it?' she asks, with an odd mixture of incredulity and warmth. 'God, he forgets everything, poor duck.'

We both look on quizzically, imploring Angie with our clueless eyes to give us more detail.

'I'm afraid we've got £3K outstanding for the booze in the social club and £2K deferred to HMRC on the VAT. You'd have thought he'd have remembered.'

'You would have,' I reply drily as I tap away frantically at the calculator, each additional press of the 'add' sign increasing the sensation of dread that is starting to overwhelm me. Dad shifts uncomfortably, waiting impatiently for my maths session to conclude.

'It's roughly a £87K shortfall per annum,' I say despondently.

'Possibly,' adds Angie, as she slurps at her tea, not content to put us out of our misery just yet. 'Twenty grand of our income comes from grant funding. We can't take that for granted – forgive the pun.'

Dad takes his phone out in exasperation and starts punching in numbers. 'So it could be as much as £107K,' he announces forcefully.

'It could be more,' Angie responds matter-of-factly, like a lion toying with its prey.

'How?' I ask, my voice now shooting up a full octave, giving me the air of an exasperated choirboy.

Angie leans back in her chair with no intention of sugar-coating the increasingly bitter pill. She opens fire, shooting terrible news at us with killer precision. We gawp at her, two well-dressed rabbits in the headlights about to be mowed down by our own lack of due diligence.

'We got relegated last season,' she reminds us. 'So we had teams like Stockport County coming here, bringing thousands. This season we'll have Bamber Bridge and Mickleover Sports visiting. No disrespect to them but we'll take less on a match day. Plus we have to join the FA Cup earlier so we're not guaranteed the same prize money.'

My head falls into my hands and I briefly entertain the idea of running away. I manage to steel myself and ask how much this new set of revelations will cost.

'Eight grand maybe,' she replies.

'Christ! It's not a gap, it's a bloody chasm!' Dad moans, mopping his sweaty head with a flannel from his bag.

We sit quietly for a moment and look around, all slightly lost for words. A pigeon coos softly outside, unaware of what's unfolding. We've gone from being comfortably in the black to well and truly in the red in the space of a five-minute conversation. To say this has taken the shine off the occasion would be an understatement. I suddenly realize what the alien expression was on Tony's face when he left. It was relief. Pure, unadulterated relief. No wonder he shot off into his office! We've been left on the *Titanic* and he's sailed off on a carpet-covered dinghy.

'We'll make it work,' Dad says bullishly, breaking the silence.

'Absolutely,' I respond, done for the day but not yet dusted. 'I mean, how hard can it be to find an extra two and a half grand a week? Get more people into the matches, sell more beer in the bar,' I offer, trailing off slightly.

'Exactly,' says Dad, glossing over the lack of detail I've offered. He slaps his hand against his knee decisively and gets up. 'We should make a move.'

We grab our coats and bags and head out. As we walk back through the main office Tony waves from across the room. To my eyes he's noticeably more buoyant and seems to be gliding around the room like a portly ice-skater.

We trudge back down the stairs towards the exit door. Just as we leave I spot another poster. This time Tony is wearing an old-school professor's hat and a smirk. Below, in the same large black font, it reads ALWAYS BE PREPARED. LINO EXCUSES.

'Touché, Tony,' I think to myself. 'Touché.'

2

Under-promise, Over-deliver

'All right, shut it!' booms our vice chairman Harry 'Robbo' Roberts at the unruly gaggle of mostly middle-aged men dotted about the social club at Hurst Cross. An expectant hush quickly settles over the room and all eyes come to rest on Dad and me.

We're sat behind a long white table on a makeshift stage formed out of flight cases and a beer crate, ready to be introduced to the club's supporters. Behind us is a loosely hung banner that reads NEW BEGINNINGS.

The social club's decor is a jumble sale of different eras. Dark oak tables are strewn with Tetley's beer mats and the deep-purple carpet smacks of the eighties. The wallpaper is floral anaglypta in tan and red. Nostalgia and an unshifting cigarette smell hang faintly in the air. You can look out of the windows and see the entire pitch on one side and rows and rows of terraced houses on the other.

On normal days the room's hum is underscored by the tinny bing-bong of a lone fruit machine, the clang of an *Open All Hours*-style till and the rhythmic thud of darts landing on their board. All syncopated by the occasional bout of indus-trial language. A television with a soft-definition focus hangs on the wall opposite the bar. The staff are referred to as stew-ards and stewardesses.

Tonight's event is moderately well attended, which I'm told by Robbo is 'by our standards very good', and will take the form of a Q&A. After feeling like I struggled at the meeting with Tony, I spent the previous evening prepping. On the table next to me are two large notebooks full of facts, stats and ver-bal prompts. Dad, who by his own admission is not a comfortable public speaker, has two pints of Dutch courage next to him and has told me to do the talking this evening. The only thing we've agreed beforehand is to tread carefully. Not to ruffle any feathers and to abide by the mantra 'under-promise and over-deliver'. Not the other way round.

I'd say there's around forty-eight people here plus one pretty ill-looking dog. Some folk look warm and friendly, others do not. They sit with folded arms, scowling at us with mistrust, and do not take off their coats. Everyone's here to find out more about who the two outsiders taking over their club are. At the back of the room are a few local journalists, including a reporter who I'm told is from the *Manchester Evening News*. I can only assume it has been a record slow news day in Greater Manchester.

Despite having performed to audiences of thousands I can't remember ever feeling quite as nervous in my life. My stomach is in knots and I'm desperate to make a good first impression. I'm also painfully aware, looking out across the room, that I am the odd one out. I'm smaller, younger and dressed differ-ently from everyone else. I feel uncomfortable and I can't shake the self-doubt that is gnawing away at me. I'm doing my best to look dynamic, which has manifested itself in me sitting up incredibly straight and opening my eyes very wide.

Robbo stands behind us. He's an incredibly tall, broad-shouldered man in his early sixties with huge hands, reminiscent of baseball gloves. He's an ex-police officer, ex-goalkeeper and current curmudgeon. From our limited interactions so far my main take-away is that he loves football but hates footballers. He believes they 'can't be trusted' and is fixated with how they maintain their kit. Some players apparently cut into the back of their socks to release the pressure on their calves. Robbo regards this as an act of vandalism. He's told me we must as a club 'come down hard' on anyone who does this and that it's 'the thin end of the wedge'.

'Let's get cracking, shall we?' he says. 'It's an exciting day for the club. We've known for a while that we need change and now it's here. I'm honoured to introduce you to Jonathan and David, our new joint chairmen.'

There's a semi-pregnant pause that's only filled by Robbo deploying his oven-mitt hands to cue a small round of applause.

'Thank you,' says Dad unsurely before nervously finishing off one of his pints and signalling for a replacement.

'Let's get on with the questions – we've all got homes to go to,' Robbo adds unceremoniously.

'Except Phil,' someone shouts from the crowd, prompting laughter from everyone except one crestfallen-looking man who I assume is Phil. I later discover Phil's recently been kicked out of his home after his wife found out he was 'having it off' with the supervisor at the Co-op.

I look down and open the first page of my notebook for reassurance and inspiration. 'Look Dynamic' it reads. I curse myself quietly and widen my eyes a little more.

'I'll kick us off,' chips in an older gentleman, wearing a navy-blue jumper and an official club tie. He's an ex-director at the club and possibly one who has been asked to take a step back to make space for me and Dad. 'Your background is in theatre. What on earth makes you think you can run a football club?'

'Steady on, Larry, we don't want to scare the boy off before he's even started,' responds Robbo, prompting a few chuckles.

It is a pretty brutal opener, and it's not made any easier to respond to by being called 'boy' just before I speak for the first time. If I'm being honest, though, it's not totally unfair and luckily I've thought about my answer already. I check my notes and begin.

'I think we'll learn a lot on the job,' I say, clearing my throat gently. 'Our role here is to look after the club and not what happens on the pitch. That's the job of the manager, right? We just need to make sure we can pay the bills and grow the club off the pitch.'

'Yes,' adds my dad heavily before returning to his second pint.

'Just don't ask me to play midfield one week,' I joke, leaving a gap for laughter that's met by a Berlin Wall of silence.

The dog whines and we share a moment of eye contact. Not ready to be beaten I sit up straighter and widen my eyes a little more.

'The point is,' I continue, 'my job isn't to get involved where others know better. It's to support those who do. I just need to have the humility to listen to those who are older and wiser than me.'

There's another even pregnanter pause. It appears my attempts to flatter Larry have not worked. He's studying me with suspicious emerald eyes and the rest of the room are watching for his verdict. For a moment I feel like an armoured gladiator waiting for the emperor's thumbs up or down on whether I'll be fed to the lions. In this case, though, I'm dressed in a preppy Ralph Lauren shirt and the lions are mildly hostile old men supping on John Smith's.

After a moment of deliberation I'm granted a stay of execution. Larry inhales sharply and says, 'We'll see, young Jonathan. Sounds nice, but nice doesn't get you anywhere in football.'

'Alrighty,' says Robbo, thankfully interrupting Larry's death stare. 'A bit heated. Next question.'

Another hand attached to a deeply sceptical face shoots up. It's Frank Taunton, an opinionated supporter in his seventies. He's spent the last week campaigning against us on Facebook. His main issue seems to be that he's against any kind of change. It's not broken so why are we letting two outsiders come and fix it? He's influential at the club though, and if only for an easy ride I've been told it's important to get him 'onside'.

'Yes, Frank,' says Robbo.

'What's the target for the team this season?' he snarls at me.

'I don't want to commit just yet,' I reply, smiling charmingly. 'I'm sure the last thing you want is me coming in here and telling you what we can do before my feet are even under the table.'

Frank sips his pint with derision and shakes his head mournfully.

I have not got him 'onside'.

A sea of hands fly up and I start to get the feeling that it might be quite a bruising evening, so I'm delighted when Angie is picked for the next question. As she's a fellow board member and club treasurer at least I'll get a bit of a softball question, I figure.

'Is there an impending financial crisis at the club?' she asks.

'No, Angie,' I say as firmly as I can. 'I think we're on a solid footing and that's not something we need to worry about.'

'Oh good. So you've sorted out all the debt?' she replies.

Dad reaches for his third pint and I feel a tidal wave of frustration building inside my stomach.

The dog growls. I know how he feels.

'Look, Angie, there's no cause for concern. No matter what the situation is we're inheriting, when we leave it'll be better than it is now.'

'When are you leaving?' yells someone at the back, sparking laughter at my expense.

'Chairboy's been frightened,' adds Phil, to roars of merriment, no doubt pleased not to be the butt of the joke for a change.

Undeterred I press on, remembering my notes and visualizing a calm version of myself. Masterful, alert and dynamic. The hands go up again and Robbo picks the next quizzer.

'What's wrong with your eyes?' asks Benji, our joint kitman.

'Moving on!' booms Robbo again.

'We should all get free club shirts!' shouts Stella, the head of the official Ashton United Supporters Club. 'I think we, the members, should all get free shirts.'

I sense this is a politically charged subject as there's a groan of frustration from a few in the crowd while others tap their glasses on the tables in approval. I wait for Stella's question but it's not forthcoming and Robbo moves us on.

'He's not answered the question, y'prick,' she protests.

'You've not asked one,' he retorts.

'Yes,' adds Dad, bewilderingly.

Another hand pops up. This time it's Bryan, who's sat with his husband Ash. They both want to know when we're 'going to sign a real goalscorer'. I don't have time or space to reply as the question is met by roars of agreement from the crowd.

I'm starting to sense the evening getting away from me. I make sure I pick the next questioner and point at a man called Tom who's sat with his daughter Bethany and brother Dennis. I know Tom from when I actually *was* a boy and he's a sound bloke. He used to take me to watch away games when Dad wasn't up for it. He's also a trustee for the club's charity that does good work in the community.

'Yes,' I say, impersonating as best I can a man in control of the situation.

'I think it's really great what you're both doing,' he begins. 'One thing that's always been a problem for the club is our attendances.'

There's a murmur of consensus from everyone, with even Larry nodding sagely, adding that it's been an issue for decades.

'We've always had a notoriously low gate,' Tom continues. 'I think last year we were stuck on about a hundred and eighty. Great if you're a darts player but not for a football crowd. Have you got a plan to turn that around?'

It's a really good question and one that, for so many

non-league clubs, is the cause of many a sleepless night. Aside from beer sales, the average gate receipt on a match day is the sole source of income and is often the difference between a club existing and not. Money is incredibly tight at the lower end of the football pyramid and a far cry from the multi-billion-pound business of the Premier League. With little to none of that money filtering down, clubs like ours rely entirely on the generous time of local volunteers, a small but madly loyal support base and the occasional bit of grant money that might trickle through.

It means clubs are locked in a near constant battle with one another for attention and attendance. Fighting it out over scraps and for the odd extra person on the terraces. I would say it is particularly grim up north in this respect. There are, to be precise, sixty-three semi-professional outfits in the Greater Manchester area alone, from Stockport County at the top of the National League (tier five) right down to Eagley FC rooted to the bottom of the West Lancashire Football League Division One (tier twelve).

Ashton United sits in the heart of Tameside, a borough that can boast a whopping seven local clubs in total. There's more non-league football teams per square kilometre than GP surgeries, fire stations and large-scale supermarkets combined. In fact, you can find a non-league football ground every few miles, and they come at a quicker frequency than the local buses. It's within this over-saturated football locality that Ashton United compete. On the field we do above averagely, with only local rivals Curzon Ashton (the blue side of town) playing at a higher level. However, when it comes to off-the-field matters we're one of the poorest and certainly least well attended.

'The honest answer is there are no easy fixes here,' I respond. 'We've got to make ourselves central to the community. For me, that means growing the charity, selling tickets electronically to get younger people engaged. We also need to have more teams, a women's first team minimum and a junior set-up. If we're going to get ahead of the pack we need to be a club for everyone.'

'Yes,' adds Dad again, now on to his fourth pint of courage and looking a little more at peace, and glassy-eyed.

'Thanks, guys,' adds Tom appreciatively.

There's a subtle but perceptible shift in the air and I spot a few people unfolding their arms. A couple even toy with the zips on their coats. I've got a long way to go but for the first time in the evening I feel like I've bought myself a little credibility. The hands go up again but I feel slightly more at ease with myself and ready for whatever might come my way.

'Next question,' calls Robbo as I relax my retinas.

Then without warning, Dad slams his pint pot down on the table.

'Can I just say something,' he interjects, wiping his mouth, looking out at everyone with defiance. 'This is Ashton United, right?'

There's an awkward silence. Nobody is sure whether to respond or not.

'The thing is, I'm listening because I'm not one for words . . . but I'm listening, and I'm thinking, we're Ashton United, right?'

I'm not totally sure where he's going and I don't think he is either, but it's clear he's had enough of sitting on the sidelines for the evening.

'We are,' I respond unsurely.

'Exactly. We are Ashton United,' he says for the third time, his lip trembling slightly. 'This club is a sleeping giant. What do you do with a sleeping giant? You wake it up!'

He passionately beats his fist against the table. I look across at him and he winks confidently. I share another moment of eye contact with the dog, who looks full of trepidation.

'This club is going to be massive with me and him in charge. We're going to have thousands in when we're done,' he says, slapping me on the back boisterously. 'I promise we will wake the giant!'

Dad leans back in his chair, and I look out across the social club to assess the damage. There's a strange hiatus while everyone catches up with the shift in rhetoric. Then, with Larry leading the way, the room bursts into applause.

I'm uncomfortable with the description of the club as a sleeping giant; it feels disconnected to reality. If anything we're a snoozing hobbit. There's no way we're going to have thousands of people here any time soon. I start to try to pedal back a little, bring us back on to an even keel.

'I think what Dad's trying to say is we're going to give everything we've got, but the growth of the club has to be sustainable. It's going to take a long time to get to—'

'I run my business like a business,' Dad interrupts, to everyone's approval except mine. For a man who doesn't like public speaking he's doing a very good impression of someone who loves it. 'I'll tell you something right now, there's no failure in me and there's no I in failure.'

'Yes,' I add, somewhat heavily.

And just like that the evening has been flipped on its head.

All my preparation undone by four pints of lager and a packet of footballing populism. The coats are off and the applause is spirited as Dad commits to more and more targets, answering each question with increasing boldness and authority. I slump deep in my chair and nurse a half pint while trying to keep up with the growing number of promises we now need to deliver on. I give up after the vow to build the 'largest electronic scoreboard ever seen at our level', 'a brand-new stand' (we can't even half fill the current one) and 'a truly unrivalled floodlight system' (whatever that means).

I'm frustrated, and cross with Dad, who has by all accounts upstaged me. Not to mention failed to stick to what we agreed to beforehand. But that's not the main problem. There's something else that's eating away at me. The truth is, I can't help but take the crowd's lukewarm response to my carefully thought-out answers and their overwhelmingly positive reaction to Dad as a rejection of me personally. It feels like the more detail and balance I have given, the less I have been listened to. Dad, meanwhile, has been embraced as one of their own. He's now talking about building a car park and children's play area and they're hanging off his every word, like the converts of an evangelist preacher. I seem to have been shunned like a politician who can't answer a direct question.

Dad might be speaking bollocks, but at least the bollocks come from his heart. As the Q&A continues I know I need to do something to change the narrative a bit. To put myself forward as someone with a vision for the club. I need to show *my* bollocks! I look down at my notes and at my half-drunk half pint, take a deep breath and begin.

'I'd just like to go back to Frank's question from earlier,' I say, cutting Dad off mid-flow. 'I *do* have a target for the season. We're here to win the league. Anything less than that is unacceptable. That's the target, Frank.'

The crowd shift in their seats a little. Frank remains impassive but there's a smattering of clapping coming from some. My heart's thumping but I ignore it and push on.

'We're not just going to win, either. We're going to win playing the best brand of football Hurst Cross has ever seen. You won't just get a goalscorer, Bryan, you'll get two. That's how we get the gate up, Tom.'

The applause builds, and a shot of adrenalin courses through me. It's Dad's turn to look on in befuddlement now. I turn to him and try to wink, but I can't, so I just kind of blink in a weird manic way and carry on pitching.

'I want us to be competitive in cups. We're long due an FA Cup run, aren't we?' I ask, prodding my finger on the table. 'We're certainly long due winning the local cup. That's the target, Frank,' I say again for added effect.

I signal dramatically to the bar for another drink and lift up my half pint which in an attempt to down in one I accidentally pour all over myself. It doesn't matter though, I'm on a roll. I plough on with an improvised list of ambitions and 'non-negotiables'. Records sure to be broken and history set to be rewritten in the coming year. Eat your heart out, unrivalled floodlight system! Up yours, electronic scoreboard! I've got my audience just where I want them. I cast my notes aside with faux nonchalance, driving towards a conclusion.

'There are no limits on what we can do together!' I hear myself shouting. 'We're going to take this club nationwide!

We're non-league now but we won't be by the time we're finished!'

Mic drop! They think it's all over . . . well it certainly is now. It's 9.30 p.m., and Robbo brings the Q&A to a close. There's a final thunderous round of applause and some even rise to their feet in appreciation, although given the average age of the room it could be down to their bladders rather than their enthusiasm. The point is that everyone is happy. Frank, Bryan, Ash, Tom and Beth look delighted. Even Phil looks full of good cheer, and why wouldn't he? If even half of what we've promised happens then we'll have ushered in a new golden age for the club.

We make our way to the bar and congratulations rain down on us from all sides. People rush over to thank us or to shake hands. They promise to buy season tickets, say that they can't wait for the season to start. I won't lie, it feels good! I feel accepted into the fold and for the moment I'm not worried about fitting in or our finances. I grab two pints and make my way triumphantly over to Dad, who has found a table in the corner away from everyone.

'Well that seemed to go well,' I beam.

'You think?' Dad says, looking pretty hacked off. 'What happened to under-promising? We've got our work cut out now.'

I look out of the window to the pitch, then across the social club. I spot Larry staring at me as he puts on his hat to leave. The dog growls and follows him out. 'Sweet Caroline' plays on the jukebox. Everybody at the bar cheers and sings in excitement for the future.

'Shit,' I think to myself. Chairboy is frightened.

39

3

Meet the Media

It's an overcast Monday morning at Hurst Cross. The sky is a milky grey and the turf is soft and muddy after a night of insistent drizzle. Three days have passed since our introduction to the fans. The few exchanges I've had with Dad have been a little terse. To be fair it's been a stressful first week and our honeymoon period at the club seems to have ended without ever really having begun.

To make matters worse, Dad has found an unofficial AUFC fans' forum online featuring a few less than complimentary threads about both of us. He's unable to stop talking about it. For a man who once boasted to me that he doesn't really 'have feelings' I'm surprised by how genuinely upset he seems. I try to pass on a bit of wisdom based on my experience of working in TV and theatre, where you're so often met with other people's opinions. Not to overthink stuff and to avoid reading negative feedback if you can. In response he wastes no time in repeating exactly what's been said about me. The criticism varies from 'He doesn't sound like he's from Ashton' to 'He's always waving his hands about when he's talking' to 'He seems

41

far too nice to be credible'. I say I don't mind and it's all water off a duck's back but of course it bothers me terribly. This duck's back is badly hurt, and now can't stop thinking about its hands.

The lion's share of the feedback comes from a man called @TheAnonymousRobin who everyone else in the chat group refers to as Neville Peterson. Neville's main gripes appear to be that neither of us committed to building an official online fans' forum and that we have moved season ticket sales online rather than buying them with cash from Frank Taunton. In Neville's defence, ticket sales so far are very low, with only three sold.

'I'm going to find him on a match day and have a word,' Dad says menacingly.

'I don't think threatening an old man on the terraces will ingratiate us with the supporters,' I retort sharply.

'I didn't say threaten,' he replies.

'What would you say to him then?' I ask.

'That for us to succeed he needs to back the leadership no matter what.'

'Like North Korea,' I offer.

'Exactly,' he responds.

I decide to ignore the comments of our Dear Leader and put the fans' forum to the back of my mind. Today there's a bigger fish to fry. I've managed to pull some strings and secure us an interview on local news show *Granada Tonight*. We'll be speaking with leading sports anchor Chris Hall for the 6 p.m. news show. It's the first time I feel like I've been able to really contribute. It's a chance to reach a wider audience and maybe even tempt some more locals to come and watch when the season starts. In short, it's an important opportunity we can't afford to waste. Dad's nerves are palpable, while I am determined not to repeat my mistakes from a few days ago. To not get carried away, and to appear grounded at all costs.

'I don't mind not doing this,' Dad says for the umpteenth time. 'This is more your sort of thing.'

'It'll be fine,' I reassure him.

'I know it will,' he responds defensively. 'I'm just not good with cameras,' he admits bashfully.

It's true. If you go through photos of my childhood there are very few of Dad where he doesn't have the air of a hostage or someone who's just been given terrible news.

'We should both do it,' I say, softening a little. 'It would be nice to do it together as father and son.'

He nods stoically. 'OK. I just don't want to end up doing something daft and everyone laughing at us.'

'Just be yourself and it will be fine,' I promise him.

The interview is a pre-record and will take place pitchside. It's sparked considerable interest from local supporters, with six fans milling around the ground to watch. Apparently it's the first time the club has been on terrestrial TV since we were briefly featured during coverage of a break-in at the local nail salon. The ground itself is often referred to as a 'proper non-league ground', which I think is a euphemism for being a bit knackered.

To be fair it's one of the oldest football stadiums in the country. It hosted its first match back in 1879 when we played under the guise of Hurst FC, and has an almost museum-like quality. It's painted in the club colours, red and white, and made mostly of breeze-block and corrugated sheet metal. The ground is surrounded by terraced houses and a church. The local attractions include a medium-sized ASDA, a Texaco garage and a banging tandoori. The official capacity is 4,500, although I can't imagine for the life of me how that many people would fit in. Inexplicably, a quick google will tell you our record attendance was 9,000! This was for a Lancashire Senior Cup match against Blackburn Rovers back in 1880. It will also tell you that the ground is most famous for its floodlights, which were installed in 1953 and used in the first ever FA-approved floodlit competition. They've remained mostly untouched ever since, meaning they haven't really worked since the late seventies.

It's a mainly open and uncovered 'arena' made up of standing-only terraces with the exception of the Sid Sykes Main Stand which seats 250 people. I have no idea who Sid Sykes is (or was) and neither does Google. There's a smaller stand behind the goal at the Rowley Street end, called the Roy Donnelly Stand, which is made out of two goal frames bolted together. Opposite the Sid Sykes Stand is the ironically named 'Popular Stand', which is always empty. It's surrounded by trees that lurch unevenly into the stadium and are the focus of many a committee meeting as they enable young kids to climb up and watch the game without paying. One tree was also once used by a supporter to defy a ban imposed by the club for lewd behaviour: the guy climbed up the tree with a megaphone and sang 'I shall not be moved', outfoxing everyone and causing much consternation during a defeat to Witton Albion.

A series of postbox-red Portakabins serve as toilets, an office, a club shop containing a mishmash of old programmes and memorabilia, and a tea hut that does pie and chips on a match day. It's all a little faded and jaded but maintained with love and an almost priestly devotion by our groundsmen Deano and Dale.

Deano is a serious man with a monotone voice who doubles up as the club's general manager. He has tight curly black hair and used to work for British Telecom. His hobbies include football and complaining. He complains mostly about football, but given the opportunity he can complain about most things. He approaches his work at the club with a steely determination, often battling against bad weather and minimal resources. He worries a lot about the condition of the grass and is locked in an on–off battle with our manager to reduce the amount of time the players are on the pitch.

Dale, on the other hand, exists in a constant state of affability. He has a shaved head, wears a club tracksuit and chain-smokes rollies like they're going out of fashion. I think he's in his sixties but his stamina makes it hard to tell. He's quite literally unable to say no to any request and has a seemingly infinite list of job titles and responsibilities at the club including club secretary, groundskeeper, assistant kitman and reserve team manager. There's also an unconfirmed rumour that in the early nineties he was once named in the starting eleven during an injury crisis. Outside the club he works as a postman. His wife Georgina runs the tea hut and his son Simon manages traffic control on a match day. It's families like Dale's and people like Deano that fuel so many non-league clubs up and down the country.

Confirmation of the TV interview came in late last night. My friend who works at Granada called me to let me know that another story had fallen through and her editor had 'no choice' but to include us. Since then Deano and Dale have worked relentlessly, painting the terraces and mowing the pitch.

They've also installed our new pitchside advertisement boards which look really smart and professional, as well as being very helpful to the general health of the club. Each board has been sold at £500 a pop, with everything other than the price of the board going directly to the club's coffers. Dad and I have managed to convince several local businesses and indeed a few non-local ones to partner up with us for the season and hopefully beyond.

I've even managed to get a few close friends and people I've worked with in the world of entertainment involved so we now have some very unique sponsors. These include several West End shows, and most impressively, we are now the only club in non-league and indeed English football that has an advertisement for a Las Vegas magic show. An ad board for Penn & Teller Live at the Rio proudly and paradoxically stands behind the goal, sandwiched between boards for a local cab rank and Bradley's Fresh Pies. It's a great story for us, though I'm not sure how many tickets we'll sell for Penn & Teller as Hurst Cross is located 5,065 miles away from the Nevada casino they call home.

'It's looking pretty damn good,' Deano shouts flatly.

We stand on the sidelines giving a thumbs up and the crowd of six applaud mildly.

It's true to say that everyone in attendance has made an effort for the big day. Dad is wearing a shirt so heavily starched he can't move, Robbo has combed the little hair he has left, while Angie is dolled up to the nines in an electric-yellow blouse. Everyone, including the grounds team, are wearing official club blazers in case they are asked to step in front of camera. I've made the rather rash decision to whiten my teeth with a kit from Boots but have arguably been a little over-zealous with the bleaching gel. Nobody seems to have noticed though, so it's maybe not as bad as I think it is.

It's only 10 a.m. and the cameras are still half an hour away. A light rain gently falls as our collective excitement for AUFC's fifteen minutes of fame grows.

After a few moments the silence is broken by Angie, who asks, 'What's wrong with your teeth, Jonathan?'

I stumble for an answer but I'm saved in the nick of time as the guest of honour arrives early.

'Hello everyone,' beams Chris.

Everyone rushes over to shake his hand, hoping they might be picked to be interviewed, except for Dad, who hangs back a little by the tea hut, hovering like a nervous schoolboy and sipping anxiously from a polystyrene cup.

'Good to meet you,' booms Robbo jovially. 'Can we get you a brew? A bacon sandwich?'

'That would be great actually!' Chris replies.

'Dale,' Robbo shouts, 'make our guest a bacon sandwich.'

'Will do,' obliges Dale, getting off his mower and heading towards the tea hut.

'I'm so pleased to be here,' says Chris. 'We should be cover-ing grassroots a lot more.'

This comment goes down very well. Chris is a natural at putting people at ease. He's an incredibly smiley man with mop-ish mousey hair and a silky TV-ready voice. He's come carrying his camera and boom and explains that today he'll be fulfilling the role of cameraman, sound op and anchor simultaneously. As he sets up he beckons to Dad, who winces and duly takes his place on the sidelines, leaning awkwardly against the metal framework of the terraces. Chris points the camera at him and the colour almost instantly drains from Dad's face. He looks incredibly uncomfortable.

'David, can we just start by saying what you had for breakfast this morning please?'

'I can't remember,' Dad panics. 'I thought we were talking about football.'

'Don't worry, it's just for sound levels,' Chris reassures him.

The interview begins, and Dad looks seriously wooden. He stares straight down the camera. The questions are all amiable but he gives off the air of a browbeaten politician under intense scrutiny, fearful of a 'gotcha moment', giving mostly yes and no answers. After a couple of minutes Chris realizes that the conversation isn't going to thaw out and moves on to ask a few closing questions.

'So, you're taking on running this club with your son?' Chris asks gently.

'Yes,' responds Dad.

'And are you looking forward to that?'

'Yes,' he says again.

'And do you have a plan for the season?'

'No,' Dad replies, suddenly looking terrified.

'No?' asks Chris.

'Yes,' says Dad, correcting himself. 'I have lots of ideas. Jonathan also has ideas but his are radical.'

'Like what?' asks Chris.

'No,' replies Dad.

'No what?' asks Chris.

'Comment,' says Dad. He leans back off the safety barrier, only to reveal a huge red paint stain across his white shirt and the palm of his hands. 'Shit!' he shouts.

'Let's cut there,' Chris suggests decisively, 'I think I've got everything I need. Who's next?'

Dale runs over and proffers our host a bacon sandwich and a tea. He gives Dad a consoling pat on the back and we all offer hollow congratulations as he shuffles back towards us. Angie strides forward buoyantly, ready for her turn, joined by Robbo.

They're both naturals in front of camera, full of life and in their own way totally at ease. Possibly too at ease in the sense that neither of them has any filter at all. Angie gives a warts-and-all account of the club's finances without even being asked while Robbo seems able only to talk about our recent relegation and how terrible the standard of football has been. At one point he describes coming to Hurst Cross as 'brutal punishment' and suggests threatening criminals with a season ticket could help cut down the reoffending rate in the area. It's a masterclass in how to deter anyone from coming. Chris, to his credit, continues to ask upbeat questions. He's come in search of a feel-good story and he's not leaving until he's got one.

'The club must be bouncing since Jonathan and David arrived?' he suggests, nodding encouragingly.

'We're not the type to get carried away,' Angie parries, knocking him back.

'We've seen enough false dawns to not necessarily trust the day,' agrees Robbo.

Not accepting defeat, Chris asks one last question: 'Do you have positive feedback on the pair so far though?'

'Absolutely,' chimes Robbo.

'Supporters can say what they want but I think they're totally trustworthy,' Angie adds.

'And credible,' Robbo interjects.

The interview ends there, and it's my turn. I'm led to the Sid Sykes Stand where I take a seat on one of the red plastic chairs. The camera starts rolling, and I get off to a terrible start. Neville Peterson, aka @TheAnonymousRobin, is living in my head rent free and I suddenly can't stop thinking about my accent, my hand movements and my general credibility. It all makes for a very odd interview. To avoid repeating the mistakes of the club Q&A I answer every question with caution, speaking only in beige footballing clichés.

'You must be delighted!' Chris prompts excitedly.

'I'm just focused on the task at hand,' I respond sternly.

'Do you have any targets at the club?'

'Only to take one day at a time.'

'Do you have a message of hope for the supporters and locals?'

'It's going to be a slow process and I'm not here to be nice,' I say before smiling with my mouth closed tightly, hiding my teeth.

'Let's stop for a second,' says Chris, becoming a little frustrated for the first time.

It's a more than fair response. I'm sure Chris was hoping to meet a group of excited non-league fanatics keen to big up their club. Instead he's hardly got a word out of us, and when he has I bet he wished that he hadn't. He looks around and leans forward towards me.

'Is everything all right, mate? My editor is expecting something uplifting, and if I'm being honest, you seem quite angry.'

I apologize and ask if we can go again, promising to give a much more positive performance. The camera's little red light goes green and I get into the spirit of things. I talk about my hopes and aspirations and my connection to the club through my grandad. I give it the hard sell and say that it's going to be an exciting period in the club's history. Essentially I make all the overblown promises I made a few nights ago. The only difference is now, instead of having announced an impossibly high bar to a sixty-seater clubhouse, I've done it to the entirety of the North West. The interview ends with me again vowing to take the club into the National League while flailing my arms and flashing my blindingly bright pearly whites.

As we trudge back across the pitch I reassure myself that this could have gone much worse. That at least we're likely to attract some new interest in the club. Then just as I start to relax a little, Chris has an idea.

'You know, just before I go it would be great to get a few fun things to mix into the interviews. Just playful stuff, you know?'

He smiles disarmingly and I find myself nodding in agreement.

'Anything to help the segment,' I reply.

It's at this point that, to my horror, I am presented with a ball. My deepest fear is about to come true.

'Maybe you could just do a few keepy-uppies for the camera and then kick the ball into the net?' Chris suggests.

'Of course,' I say.

The camera's popped up on a tripod and I'm suddenly transported back to secondary school and being picked last in PE. And, of course, that scarring week at summer school. A memory of one kid's parent shouting at our coach that 'letting him play isn't fair on the other boys' springs vividly to mind, and the final session of that summer when we were told the class wouldn't finish until we had all completed five keepy-uppies in front of our peers.

I hold the ball uneasily in my hands, aware that everyone in the ground is watching. It's a small audience but I'm frozen by their gaze. I bounce the ball on my foot and lose control of it immediately, prompting a few laughs. I try again, my toe catching the ball awkwardly this time and knocking it away from me.

'Don't worry,' Chris says gently, 'I'll keep rolling until you get five.'

I keep trying. Dad, Angie and Robbo come over and start giving me tips – an on-the-spot class in close control. It is all very triggering. I can hear the voices of the children in my class begging to go home.

No matter what, I just can't do it.

'Never mind, Chairboy,' shouts someone from the stand.

'He's trying his best, Neville,' someone hisses back.

I persevere, hopelessly aware that my credibility is at an all-time low. Eventually Dad chips the ball up for me and I manage a few badly coordinated kick-ups before booting the ball out of the ground. Chris puts me out of my misery, telling me 'we can move on', before promising to cut out from the final film the twenty minutes of me failing.

'The section is only four minutes max anyway,' he consoles me.

My resistance broken, I'm taken around the stadium to film more 'light-hearted moments'. This includes a trip to the home dressing room, where I perform a deeply humiliating mock team talk to the empty benches, where all I can think of is to shout 'Let's go, boys!' on loop, and attempt a cringe-worthy slow-motion walk through the tunnel. We finish with footage of Dad and me walking up and down the pitch point-ing and gesturing vaguely, with Dad wrapped tightly in a jacket trying to hide the huge paint stain on his stomach. After what feels like an eternity of traversing the turf with faux pur-pose, Chris declares he has 'everything he needs'. Relieved, we scurry to the exit to see him off.

'So great to meet you all,' Chris says again. 'The section will be out tonight at 6 p.m. Do tune in.'

With that he packs up and heads off. The crowd of six dis-perses and everyone goes about their day. Dale and Deano head back on to the grass, Angie drives off to work and Robbo goes into the club office to shuffle some paperwork about. I look up towards the Sid Sykes Stand and briefly see the spec-tre of Larry shaking his head dolefully. He catches my eye before hobbling off with his dog in tow.

Dad and I are left in the drizzle, underscored by the distant hum of Dale's mower.

'Do you think people are going to laugh?' asks Dad grimly.

'Maybe,' I reply. 'Maybe.'

4

Going Through Changes

Two weeks have passed since the club was featured on *Granada Tonight* and we're now hurtling towards mid-June. I woke up yesterday keen to do something positive and impactful so I decided to order and pay for all the club's new kits and training equipment for the forthcoming season. This includes our home and away strips for both of our first teams and our training wear plus kitbags. Unfortunately Dad had decided to do the same so we now have double everything that we need and have paid twice as much as we should have done. I mentioned this to Angie to see if she thought we might be able to get a refund. She told me the suppliers definitely won't give us one and that at the end of last season she had also ordered kit and equipment for the forthcoming year too. So we have three times the amount of kit that's needed, plus half of an invoice from last year that's still to be settled. I later received an email from our supplier saying that due to an administrative error we've been sent an extra unit of socks meaning that around 320 pairs will arrive at the club next week. I called Deano to check if we had storage space. He informed me that the changing room is full to bursting and that we don't need to order any new kit because there's 'nothing wrong with last year's or indeed the kit used in any of the three seasons before'. He said that 'we keep wasting money on new kit' and he hopes that will stop now we're at the club and 'everyone will be more careful about what they order'. I've promised him that will certainly be the case going forward. At a rough estimate, including the recently ordered shirts and shorts, I think we now have roughly 500 kits and 650 pairs of socks for the coming season. In the changing room we have two modestly sized cupboards that are already pretty full. Angie has suggested we might sell some of the shirts to supporters. We apparently sold six last season.

When I returned home I found an email from Robbo letting me know he's had a grant application accepted from the FA for £3,000. The income is conditional: it can only be spent on kit and equipment for the upcoming season and must be used within the next four months.

Season ticket sales remain stubbornly stuck on fourteen. The ire of Neville Peterson – @TheAnonymousRobin – has not been quelled and our decision to repaint the rusty barriers on the terrace the same colour they already were has been labelled 'disrespectful to the club's traditions'. An unhelpful rumour has been circulated that I'm intending to remove John Smith's from the taps at the bar. This has prompted a small grassroots campaign called 'Mitts off my Smiths' organized by some of the older club regulars.

Dad has become obsessed with building an outdoor bar for match days. He tells everyone (whether they're interested or not) that it'll be 'easy money for the club'.

I've been inundated by applications to manage our newly formed women's team, which is great, but I have no idea how to identify a good candidate. I've picked a shortlist based entirely on the neatness and layout of the applicant's CV.

Today we're back in the clubhouse, meeting our men's first team manager Jamie Benshaw. It's a Thursday afternoon and the place is empty. Just the three of us, plus the head 'stewardess' Penny and ex-director and lifelong fan Larry. Penny stands behind the bar washing glasses, looking wistfully at the door, either dreaming of more customers or of leaving early. Larry sits at his usual table near the dartboard, walking stick balanced against the wall, nursing a whisky and a book of sudoku. The dog, Winston, sleeps.

After a rough introduction to non-league and club politics I'm delighted finally to be chatting about the beautiful game itself. We've met to go over pre-season arrangements, our ambitions for the campaign and, most importantly, recruitment. As per, I've spent an inordinate amount of time swotting up so that I can contribute to the meeting. I've listened to every podcast out there. I've read up on the importance of the high press, rotating full-backs and the role of the false nine in modern football. My aim is to come across as a studious chairman. A chairman who listens and supports but who everyone readily agrees 'really knows his stuff'. Dad has shown up with a notepad on which he has written the words *four-four-two* and *strong spine*. I feel like Pep Guardiola going out for dinner with Big Sam. Or Klopp off for a pint with Felix Magath (he was the guy who managed Fulham and suggested a player rub his leg with cheese to get over an injury).

Jamie is a charismatic chap who's great company but quick

to anger. He's early forties, dressed in an official club tracksuit, and has a rough mop of blond hair. After a career spent mostly as a free-scoring non-league striker this is his first job in management. Having initially stepped in as caretaker-player-manager (when our original guy got the hump and walked out), he's now five years in. He's done really well for us, taking us up to the dizzy heights of the Vanarama National League North via the play-offs. It was our first and only visit to tier six so despite our immediate relegation last season we've decided it would be foolish to change a manager who's previously delivered above expectations.

Determined to be on the front foot I kick the meeting off, making a concerted effort to regurgitate as many football buzz words as I possibly can. I discuss playing through the lines, the counter press, the high press and, of course, our need to be able to attack the low block. Jamie and Dad look at me nonplussed. I know I've said all the right things but not necessarily in the right order. I feel less Klopp and more Flopp as I sit in the self-created stilted silence. Eventually Jamie brings up item one on his agenda: the changing rooms.

'I want to swap the home and away changing rooms,' he says with an air of trepidation. 'The away one has better showers and doesn't smell like damp.'

'Fine,' replies Dad matter-of-factly.

Jamie seems surprised. I get the feeling he was expecting resistance, but it sounds like a very uncontroversial request.

'How, though?' he quizzes, his face full of worry.

'Just go in the away one rather than the home one?' I say with a shrug.

Jamie explains that it's not that simple. There's only one

person in the entire club who has the keys to the changing rooms. It's not the manager, the kitmen, the grounds team or even Robbo. It's club veteran and stalwart Frank Taunton.

'He won't allow it,' Jamie informs us.

It turns out that he's been asking Frank to change the rooms every season he's been manager. It's become a hot-button issue. In fact, three years ago the button became so hot that Frank changed all the locks and only made one key to ensure that no one other than him could open the changing rooms. Sometimes this has meant that players and coaching staff have arrived at the ground and found they've been unable to change until just before kick-off. There was even one fabled occasion, we're told, when Frank went on holiday to Aberystwyth and still wouldn't relinquish control of the key. This resulted in our team and the entire Blyth Spartans squad being forced to change together in the tunnel.

'That's madness,' I say.

'It's his domain,' Jamie responds balefully.

'It's not any more,' snaps Dad. 'It's mine.'

I cough.

'Ours,' he corrects.

'Why doesn't he want to swap the changing rooms?' I ask.

'The washing machine's in the home room,' Jamie says. 'Frank's worried the away team might rob it.'

'After a match?' I remark incredulously.

'Yeah. He thinks they could run out with it and put it on their coach,' Jamie responds, shaking his head.

'Unbelievable!' Dad says.

'I know,' says Jamie. 'Nobody would do that. Plus it weighs

half a ton and it's always leaking. That's why the room smells of damp.'

Dad bites down on his lip. He's not a man blessed with a surplus of patience at the best of times. He promises Jamie that by the end of the week the rooms will have been swapped, come what may, and on top of that commits to a paint job and supplying the room with new benches and a flatscreen TV to go over tactics pre-match. 'I work in construction so it's what I do,' he says with a sense of finality. 'I'm building an outside bar for match days too,' he adds. 'It's going to be easy money for the club.'

Jamie is reassured, and the conversation moves away from changing rooms and on to the pitch. We discuss our promotion-winning season and our subsequent drop back down. We're both really keen to hear Jamie's experiences over the last five years. What's worked and what's not and how the club can better support him. I also want to know more about why our turnover of players was so high last year. We seemed to have a pretty fixed first eleven during the season we went up but after that the team changed more than a Claudio Ranieri side on speed.

Jamie nods wearily, puffing out his stubbled cheeks. He ducks down from his chair, takes out a thick ring-bound folder from his sports bag and drops it on the table with a thud.

'They were all non-contracts,' he says with a hint of fury. 'The club's always had a small budget and I've not been allowed to have any players on contract. So when we went up, better clubs poached them all.'

I nod unsurely, as does Dad. Jamie spots that we need a bit

of a tutorial and starts to give us an idiot's guide to the Wild West world of non-league football recruitment. I have to say, it's a workplace like no other! For those as out of the know as I was, here is a quick breakdown of how it all works.

Some players have contracts with their clubs. They're official employees and are on the payroll and are paid PAYE. Meaning the club pays the players' tax and National Insurance contributions. Pretty standard stuff. The benefit for the player here is that they have fixed employment and a regular income regardless of injury or falling out of the starting line-up. The benefit for the club is that the player is theirs and if a bigger club wanted his services they would have to agree a transfer fee.

The other option is the player is registered as a 'non-contract player'. This is a far more relaxed form of employment where the player is most likely being remunerated on a pay-if-you-play basis. Players can be paid anything from hundreds of pounds per performance to a few quid for expenses in a brown envelope. Jamie even tells us a story of a team a few leagues below us paying their squad in meat! Their manager was a butcher so he'd sort them out with his own produce, creating a very literal take on the phrase 'bringing home the bacon'.

The advantage for a player without a contract is that he's free to leave whenever he wants. If a better option comes along all he needs to do is put in fourteen days' notice and he's free to jump ship. The upside for the club is that 'non-contracts' lower their overheads and financial risk. Especially if you're paying in pork chops.

All this means there's a huge disparity between clubs not

just in budgets but also in terms of a guarantee that they won't lose their entire first eleven en masse with just two weeks' notice. Jamie tells us the club wasn't ready for promotion. 'We weren't expecting to go up so we didn't know how to plan when we did. The main focus was getting the ground up to league standard to avoid an automatic relegation,' he tells us with frustration in his eyes. 'It's a shame because we had such a good group but I just couldn't keep them.'

Jamie gives us a blow-by-blow through a tough season during which he was constantly calling in favours just to cobble a team together. Often naming himself and his coaching staff on the bench to make up the numbers. Months of drafting in last-minute loanees from clubs on the morning of matches. Regular occasions when the first time these players met each other was in the changing room. He looks physically pained when he talks about some of the more bruising defeats and the challenges of having such little funding available.

'Some weeks we were playing against full-time teams! We were like lambs to the slaughter. We played Stockport County in front of 7,000 people and we had twenty-four away fans. I'd never met our goalkeeper until we got to the car park!'

He looks around to check nobody is listening, then motions us to come closer before confiding, 'I don't think Tony actually wanted us to go up. When we won the play-off we were all celebrating and he was stood there like someone had pissed on his shoes.'

'Why?' I ask.

'Because you'd look upset if someone pissed on your shoes,' Jamie explains.

'No, why was he upset when we went up?'

'The extra cost of travel in the league above,' he replies, getting quite worked up. 'His first words to me after we won were that we'd have to drive to Boston ourselves next year. He's tight as cramp.'

'He pays for the coaches on the quiet to be fair,' says Dad, outing Tony again.

Jamie continues monologuing, reliving heavy defeat after heavy defeat, awful refereeing decisions and the sinking morale as the inevitable drew closer. I have to admit I'm exhausted just listening. It sounds like an incredibly depressing nine months.

'Football's a fickle game,' Jamie says, full of indignation. 'One minute you're a hero and the next you're a villain. The supporters thought I was the one getting rid of everyone! I got us promoted on a shoestring and by the end of last season they were ready to hang me with it!'

Desperate to soothe Jamie I find myself reassuring him that this season will be different. As well as the increased budget, I pledge we will also contract the entire squad.

'All of them?' he says suddenly, snapping out of his malaise.

'Of course,' I say, again without really thinking.

In the corner of my eye I spot Larry looking up from his puzzle and single malt and feel his eyes burn into me. I do my best to ignore the sinking feeling in my stomach.

'That's brilliant,' says Jamie.

'Sounds good,' agrees Dad, clapping his hands together.

Jamie starts flipping through the ring binder, which turns out to be a kind of little black book. A sort of self-made Rolodex full of players' names, positions, current clubs and their contact details.

Our tutorial continues as Jamie explains that there are three kinds of player in non-league: young players who've been let go by pro clubs who are now trying to play their way back up the leagues; experienced ex-pros past their best falling down the leagues; and then, finally, lads who have found their level and circulate around different local clubs opting for whoever can offer them a package that best supports their life outside football. Non-league clubs are mostly part-time, training twice a week (Tuesday and Thursday) and playing on a Saturday, so something like the location of training can be a real deal maker.

He says that if we're doing proper contracts then it really takes us up to the 'next level'. It means we can cherry-pick the best players from those three categories and that we'll be able to put an exciting side together, full of highly talented young players, players with hundreds of league football appearances on their CV, plus the best local players in our area.

'We're going to get lads who will drop down just to play for us,' he says with relish, still thumbing through page after page of his dossier.

Dad looks delighted, and we share a moment of satisfaction. It's the first time in a few weeks we've been able to look forward to the coming season. This is after all why we've got involved. To be part of a game we love and to do our town proud. We agree that the best course of action is to act decisively and quickly, to identify our top targets and sign them now while everyone else is still in holiday mode. We'll be weeks ahead and everyone will be chasing us for the rest of the season.

It's one of our first major decisions at the club, and it feels great. We've come up with a plan that's going to attract top-quality players plus we're providing security for everyone who's playing for us. It's certainly a financial risk, but if it pays off it will put us on the map. Besides, Dad's convinced the outdoor bar will do a lot of the heavy lifting and contracting the players doesn't cost more necessarily. It just means all our overheads will be fixed for the year and we'll have no wriggle room. I push this to the back of my mind where the rest of my increasing sense of terror lives and briefly allow myself to imagine other clubs talking about us in years to come. Praising how we reshaped lower-league football. Holding AUFC as the gold standard and our leadership as the template for how to run a club!

We're going to be full of ambition, full of goals and capable of winning the league at a canter. It's going to be fantastic.

We raise our glasses.

Larry shuffles out, shaking his head. Winston follows. Penny watches as the door slams shut.

We grin and toast the inevitably successful journey ahead. It's going to be a piece of cake.

How little we knew.

5

Cashton United

Four more weeks have passed. It's now July, and pre-season has begun in earnest. It's somehow been simultaneously an incredibly eventful month and one in which not much has happened at all.

The home and away dressing rooms have not been swapped. After a robust 'exchange' of views with Dad, Frank Taunton has gone AWOL with the key. This means neither dressing room is currently operational.

We're still serving John Smith's at the bar and the 'Mitts off my Smiths' campaigners have claimed a hard-won victory. The fact that we never intended to take it off the taps is an irrelevance. Sales of John Smith's remain low. Neville Peterson continues to 'anonymously' rally for an official fans' forum by using the unofficial fans' forum which, to all intents and purposes, acts as an official fans' forum. Larry is still working through his sudoku book and seems almost omnipresent. Winston looks iller by the day. I still do not know who Sid Sykes is, or was.

Work on the outdoor bar has begun and so far it hasn't

been 'easy money'. It has been hard work and expensive. The trickiest issue has been connecting the outdoor bar to the beer line in the club. During this process the indoor bar got drenched by a vicious spray of highly pressurized lager. We now need to redecorate the indoor bar, which we will subsidize with the sales from the outdoor bar. Once we have of course recouped the costs of making the outdoor bar.

In more exciting news a huge raft of players have arrived at the club. Based on our conversation last month Jamie has opted for experience over youth. The majority of players he's signed are proven winners at or above this level. This includes two players from the National League plus Jono Hunt, the captain of our bitter foes Curzon Ashton. We've signed Jono for £2,000. I'm told this is a record club signing and his arrival has set a niche corner of social media alight. Our supporters are delighted while rival fans are furious and have dubbed us 'Cashton United'.

We certainly seem to have got the attention of players in the Greater Manchester area. Jamie is constantly on the phone to an ever-growing number of them, all of whom are desperate to join the club. Each player better and more exciting than the last, each one stretching the budget more and more. We've also got an exciting young triallist with us who Jamie is keen to bring into the fold. Unlike a lot of lads who represent themselves, though, this guy has an agent so Jamie has asked if I can call him and try to sort a deal.

I keep reminding myself that it's all a calculated risk: an immediate promotion will mean bigger clubs visiting and bringing much larger attendances. We just need to make sure we hit the ground running and everything will be fine.

Despite the buzz, season ticket sales remain stuck on fif-teen. I've been disappointed about this. Robbo tells me that this is a record number of sales for us. I've not dared ask if he means a record high or low.

All applicants from my shortlist for the women's first team manager have been snapped up by other clubs or are no longer interested. I've quickly created a new shortlist and intend on conducting interviews by the end of the week.

Today we're at the ground watching the new team being put through their paces. Jamie stands on the centre circle holding a clipboard, lambasting anyone falling behind during a series of drills. His assistant, Sandy, plays good cop and shouts encouragement. Deano chases after the players, refill-ing divots in the pitch with a rake in real time. Muttering under his breath. At one point I think he even shouts 'Be careful!' I wonder for a second if our bad form last season came from all the players focusing on trying to preserve the pitch rather than win games.

I'm sat next to Dad on the front row of the Sid Sykes Stand along with Angie and Robbo, enjoying the sun. Angie covers herself liberally in factor 50 while Robbo comments on the condition of different players' socks with increasing irritation. He says that it's 'beyond a joke' and 'a drain on our resources'. I assure him that finding replacement socks won't be an issue this year, or most likely for the next decade. He lets me know that he took the liberty of putting the recent grant money to good use and has bought just shy of a grand's worth of socks so that we have replacements.

'You'll be surprised by how quickly we burn through them,' he declares.

I smile while trying to calculate how much it's going to cost to store the tumult of sporting hosiery we're fast accruing.

Penny hovers by the bins, finishing a cigarette. Larry sits at the back with a younger woman (early sixties) who I am told is both his podiatrist and lover. Since I've learnt this I can't help but wonder which she was first. There's also a guy I don't know sat on the other side of the stand in a buttoned-up shirt, holding a pair of crutches. I think he's one of our scouts.

Our club secretary, reserve team coach, community organizer, first-aider and co-groundsman are stretched. The problem being that they are all one person – Dale. He's locked away in the club office desperately trying to get on top of everything. The sharp increase in new faces, and with them contracts, has created a flurry of paperwork that's hard to keep track of. Especially if you're also trying to do a full-time job on top of all this. To make matters worse, he's agreed to take on a new position at the club as temporary turnstile operator (until Frank Taunton reappears). I've tried to draft in Bethany (from the Q&A) to help but it turns out the only thing Dale won't agree to do is delegate.

Despite his dedication to the club he and Jamie have been butting heads. The long and the short of it is that Jamie complains that Dale forgets everything he's told and Dale complains that Jamie doesn't tell him anything. Dad also hates to email so tends to field questions on the phone on a one-on-one basis, meaning nobody knows what has been discussed or agreed (including me). To rectify this I have set up different WhatsApp groups for each department. This has been a mistake on my part. There is now a nonsensical number of WhatsApp groups each made up of the same people in slightly altered combinations, creating an overflow of incessant information and conversation. They ping almost constantly from morning until night, and sadly sometimes through the night too. The worst group is called 'AUFC Club Bins' which has quickly become the bane of my life. The conversation is focused on a mystery local who keeps breaking into the ground to use our bins for their personal rubbish. Deano has become obsessed and has set up secret cameras to nail the culprit.

Dad and Robbo keep remarking on how strong the team looks. I agree when they say we look 'proper dangerous'. Secretly I have no idea though. I find it impossible to identify a good footballer just from watching a training session. The only player I have an opinion on is our goalkeeper, the man nicknamed Tarantula. I asked him why he's called that. He told me it's because he's 'so good' it's like he's got 'eight hands' but Jamie told me it's because 'he has weird tiny hairs all over his body'. In either case I have my doubts about him and have seen him practically throw the ball into his own net several times. I've quietly voiced my concerns to Jamie who says he just needs 'a good pre-season under his belt'. Apparently he has been coaxed out of retirement.

Despite the workload it's pleasing to see a growing sense of optimism in the camp. Especially a camp that often seems wedded to the religion of pessimism at all costs. Things are due to get even better too. Later we are meeting our secret weapon – a striker called Boothy, who is a proven goalscorer. Jamie's described him as the missing part of the puzzle. We've seen a series of YouTube recordings of him via the recruitment WhatsApp, and he's definitely impressive. He's arriving after training to sign on the dotted line.

Dad and I are also planning to speak to the players after training to introduce ourselves properly. We're just not quite sure where we'll do this yet. We can't get into the changing rooms, half of the social club is covered in lager, and the other half is being used for a wake. I have no idea why but we are the go-to place in town for wakes. I suggested that we could also host weddings and Penny laughed in my face.

'Last ten now!' yells Jamie with added fury.

'Brilliant, boys, brilliant!' adds Sandy as the lads run back and forth.

The lads begin their last push, working on one-twos and one-touch passing. I notice a few of them are starting to tire. Especially Jono, who I think it's fair to say still needs to 'shift some pre-season timber'.

Sandy bounds over to us, jumping the advertising boards like Bambi – if Bambi were a middle-aged man who often said 'a positive attitude is the key that unlocks all doors'.

'Hello, gents,' he begins. 'Gaffer's just asked what the sitch is with the changing rooms today.'

I start to apologize when Dad interrupts. 'All sorted,' he answers bluntly.

'Is it?' I ask.

'Is it?' repeats Sandy. 'Because we couldn't get in on Tuesday and the lads really need to shower off.'

'Just crossed wires,' Dad promises. 'It's done.'

Sandy runs off again and speaks to Jamie. They both look over to us and give a friendly wave. Dad and I return the gesture.

I've started to be able to work out when Dad is feeling under pressure. He purses his lips slightly. It's the first warning to

72

give him space. The second is that he becomes more monosyl-labic and unwilling to engage in conversation. The third is that his face looks like a beetroot. I'm not surprised when my question as to how we'll get into the changing rooms is met by his face puckering slightly and the simple words 'working on it'. He starts texting frantically. My phone pings a few times which leads me to conclude he is using the 'Changing Rooms' WhatsApp group. It's a group with me, Dad and Frank in it. Frank has yet to respond.

I explain the situation to Angie and Robbo. That we'd promised to switch the changing rooms but since floating the idea with Frank we've not been able to find him.

'Good luck with that,' chuckles Robbo.

'Those rooms are Mr Taunton's domain,' says Angie. 'It'll be a cold day in hell before he gives them up.'

Dad grimaces and lets out an angsty-man grunt, his face turning purple. I check my phone. *Frank Taunton has left the group.* We've been ghosted by a seventy-three-year-old man and in the process locked out of part of our own football club.

Dad has had enough. He suddenly bolts down the tunnel. Robbo and Angie look on mystified and I peg it after him as fast as I can. He runs full pelt into the changing room door, knock-ing it clean off the hinges and on to the floor. He's taken back control. He's invaded Frank's domain and made it his own.

'Sorted,' he says, clearly very pleased with himself.

'This is the home dressing room,' I say.

'What?' he replies, dusting himself down.

'We're supposed to be swapping the rooms. If we wanted to be in here Frank would've just let us in. We should've broken into the away room.'

Dad's face turns a darker purple. 'I'll do that later,' he snaps dismissively.

'You're going to smash through the other room too?'

'Yes, I'll smash through that door. Then replace both doors and then change the locks and swap the rooms round for Jamie.'

'OK,' I say, deciding not to point out that we could just change the locks without breaking down and replacing the doors.

The room is very basic. Big grey breeze-block walls and some black painted wooden benches, an open-plan shower seasoned with specks of blue mould. There are a few bits of discarded kit and training equipment strewn about as well as a small white-board. An almost romantic football smell hangs in the air, a thick cologne of emotion, sweat, mud and competition. Or it could just be damp. In the corner stands the biggest washing machine I've ever seen in my life.

There's no more time for conversation or reflection, though, as we're interrupted by the sound of studded boots bouncing along the concrete floor of the tunnel. Training is over and the players are coming to shower off. Dad runs out and waves the lads in. They slump down on the benches, sweating and pant-ing heavily, ready to hear from the gaffer.

Jamie strides in authoritatively. He goes to slam the door before realizing it's gone. 'I knew it couldn't be changed,' he sneers as he bursts past us. 'Sit down!' he screams at the already fully seated squad.

Considering we haven't even played our first friendly yet, I'm surprised to see Jamie lay into everyone so harshly. He criticizes the team's attitude, their intensity and their will to win. He also criticizes somebody's haircut and makes it very clear that everyone is expected to hit a high level very quickly when we play Droylsden on Saturday.

'The whole town will be judging you!' he adds, wagging his finger for dramatic effect.

Jamie is clearly not a man who bottles up how he feels, and how he feels is mostly very angry. Whether he's reflecting on previous events, doing a deal with a player or running training, a red mist seems to doggedly follow him wherever he goes. So it's no surprise to see him losing his rag. That said, I've started to hope at least some of his rage is in some way performative. That it's a well-considered tactic to keep players and those around him on their toes.

He boots a load of drinks bottles in the corner and finishes by telling everyone that they're a 'fucking disgrace' before storming out and leaving Sandy to pick up the pieces.

'Boys, you've heard the gaffer,' he says with an earnest expression on his face. 'What he's saying is, we believe in you. We back you 110 per cent. Let's make a statement at the weekend. Remember, a positive attitude is the key to unlock all doors.'

The team applauds and the team talk is over. Personally I think Sandy's interpretation of Jamie's words is very generous. I'm not sure how you spin 'you're an embarrassment to your families' into a declaration of faith but it seems to have done the trick. The players seem happy and the bad cop, good cop routine has worked.

'Before you shower, lads, the chairmen want to say a few words,' Sandy adds as everyone starts to stir.

Dad and I take our place in the middle of the changing

room. Jamie re-enters the fray, hovering moodily by the washing machine.

'Hello. I'm David, I'm the chairman,' Dad says.

I cough.

'Co-chairman,' he corrects. 'I just want to get one thing clear, all right? From Saturday you will be changing in the away dressing room. Do not doubt it.'

It's clear from the players' faces that they know nothing about the recent request to swap the changing rooms. They all look incredibly confused.

Our new captain Jono raises his hand.

'Why?' he asks.

'Because this is my domain,' Dad responds emphatically.

'Do the home team always change in the away room here?' Jono asks.

'The away room is the home room!' Jamie yells over the washing machine.

'So why is it called the away room?' asks Tarantula.

'It won't be by Saturday,' Dad says, turning a deep shade of magenta. 'We will back you, lads. We will back you. Thank you.'

Dad gives way for me to have my turn. I clear my throat and survey the room doubtfully. Over the last few weeks I've spent more time out of my comfort zone than in it, but as I stand in the centre of the dressing room I've never felt more uncomfortable in my life. I can feel my mouth drying and my tongue feels twice its normal size. I take a deep breath, and begin.

'It's great to meet you,' I hear myself say, voice breaking as though I've just entered puberty. 'This is a talented squad and I have no doubt we're in for a fantastic season. If anyone ever has any questions about anything, our door is always open.'

There's a brief moment of thoughtful silence. The squad nods. Jono raises his hand once again.

'Where do we change for away matches?' asks another player. 'In the home room?'

Dad's face goes full magenta and Jamie looks like he might explode. The squad laughs. Sandy applauds enthusiastically and the lads join in, although some look pretty bewildered.

Just as everyone starts to move there's a knock on the wall in lieu of the door.

'Enter!' shouts Jamie, his mood souring by the second.

It's the scout from the stand. He stands unsurely at the entrance to the room, holding on to his crutches.

'Hiya,' he says in a thick Liverpudlian accent. 'I wasn't sure where to go?'

'Can we help you, pal?' asks Sandy.

'I'm Boothy,' he says, hobbling towards us. 'The new striker.'

'Bollocks,' says Dad.

6

Not So Friendly

Dad and I have been summoned to the ground early this morning by the 'grounds team'. Apparently the pitch is starting to dry up in the heat and with no rain in over two weeks the water tank that attaches to the sprinklers is taking too long to refill to guarantee we'll be able to water the grass before kick-off. It's Wednesday and the first match of the 2019/20 season is still three days away so we don't really understand how this can be possible.

Upon arrival we're taken to the plastic 10,000-gallon tank that sits behind the goal at the Rowley Street end right next to the Roy Donnelly Stand (i.e. the two goal frames draped in aluminium sheet). The issue as to why it's taking so long immediately becomes clear. We don't have any of the necessary equipment to do it. The pitch has no undersoil irrigation to collect rainwater, nor do we have a pressure pump or specialist valve to speedily refill from an exterior source. Instead, a small domestic hose has been stuck to the top of the tank with gaffer tape.

We follow the lead of the hose to find it connected to the

tap in the tea hut. Assuming we were to leave the tap on until the tank was completely full it would take a minimum of five days. Apparently, this has been done before. Nobody, including the new joint chairmen of the club, has any ideas on how to quickly fill the tank without spending a fortune the club doesn't have. We resolve to pray for rain until anyone has a better idea.

It's been a tricky few weeks. We're now just days away from the start of the new campaign and our pre-season form has been poor. It started brightly enough with a comfortable 4–2 home victory over local rivals Droylsden, but since then we've failed to record a single victory in five attempts.

A creditable draw against league club Oldham Athletic was followed by four consecutive defeats, including a 1–0 loss to Fleetwood under-21s, a disastrous 3–0 hammering by Colne FC during a morale-lowering team bonding weekend, plus a humbling defeat against another of our many local rivals, AFC Mossley, who walked to a 2–0 victory. This was topped off by a 3–1 loss to Chester where we had to do without our promising young midfielder Dodsey after he was convinced by his teammates that, because he hadn't brought his passport, he'd have to hide in the boot of their car to smuggle himself across the border into Wales. I'm told it was all 'just banter' until the boot got jammed and Dodsey had to spend the entire ninety minutes in the foetal position inside the bowels of a Nissan Micra.

Our uninspired pre-season form hasn't helped season ticket sales either, which have now peaked at thirty-two. Although really it's only thirty-one because I bought one of them for myself. My mum also bought two, and my grandad bought one, so I suppose they don't count either. We also received an email from a man asking for a refund because he'd meant to buy a ticket for another Ashton United based in Bristol. So most likely the final count is twenty-seven.

Off the field, Deano has identified the phantom bin user. After a careful review of grainy CCTV footage and a one-man stakeout the culprit turned out to be vice chairman Robbo. Robbo had recently sorted out his garage and couldn't be bothered driving to the tip. This has caused a mini conflict within our board and the two have 'had words'. Deano believes Robbo using the bins for his own personal use is 'an abuse of power' while Robbo feels Deano is being 'a bit of a dick about the whole thing'.

I spoke to our triallist's agent. He goes by the name of 'Flash' and he certainly has an unconventional approach. He says he got his nickname because of 'the speed of his negoti-ation skills'. He started by demanding huge sums of money, saying his client was destined for the Premier League, but very quickly accepted £125 per week and a £5 goal bonus. Con-cerningly, once we'd agreed terms, he asked me if the player he represented was actually any good. He said he takes on so many clients 'it's impossible to watch all of them' and that he favours 'a throwing spaghetti at a wall' approach, as opposed to traditional scouting.

Frank Taunton has returned from his brief one-man boy-cott but isn't speaking to either Dad or me, such is his disgust at what we've done to the changing rooms. He's taken to the unofficial fans' forum to officially brand the move as 'despotic'.

Although I am not making many friends at the moment I

have finally managed to appoint a women's first team manager. Her name is Debby and she's the only person at the club
with a UEFA A coaching badge, making her the most quali-
fied person here. Unfortunately we have no squad and only
four players turned up to our first and second trial sessions.
Debby's been very clear that she has no time to drive the
recruitment process and can only commit to training whoever
turns up. This leaves us with a month to cobble together a full
squad before the Greater Manchester Women's League starts,
otherwise we forfeit our league deposit and more money will
disappear into the football-shaped black hole that is starting
to engulf my bank account. We've posted almost constantly
on Twitter and Facebook asking for talented players to get in
touch, or indeed just players – at this point we can't afford to
be picky. So far we've received only one reply, from one of the
four original potential players letting us know that she's no
longer interested in playing for us. I have no doubt we look
incredibly desperate and there's now a lot of doubt as to
whether we'll find an eleven before the deadline.

Despite the bumpy start for our men's team on the pitch,
I've been reassured by our manager and his staff that pre-season isn't about the results. Sandy has reminded me frequently
that 'it's the team's performance that counts' at this stage and
'not the final score'. I'd find this comforting if I didn't secretly
think the performances have been much worse than the results.
Maybe it's just nerves as the season approaches but I've started
to feel an increasing sense of worry about our squad.

Our goalkeeper seems to have a genuine aversion to stopping goals. The more match practice he gets the more erratic
he becomes. Our defence appears slow and our strikers are

less lethal than a lethargic stingray on Xanax. Some of our players don't seem to be getting fitter either, and although we look good on the ball we don't seem that interested when we're out of possession. We're also starting to make a habit of conceding late goals as well as early ones, and quite a few in the middle of games too. Our star striker Boothy still hasn't played. He's off the crutches now but yet to feature on the pitch, other than walking gingerly from the sidelines to the tea hut at half-time.

Given how many new players we have who are playing together for the first time, I'm also surprised by how many of them have had to miss matches due to being on holiday. This includes our manager Jamie who, after pestering us to fund the disastrous team bonding trip, was unable to take part in most of the bonding because he had to catch an early-morning flight to Tenerife. A big part of me feels I should confront him about this but an even bigger part of me feels I am very scared of Jamie and it's best not to mention it. I'm also aware that most people have a full-time job so it's probably unreasonable to expect everyone to be at every match?

I've tried to broach some of these concerns with Dad in recent weeks but he's doggedly refused to engage with anything that he perceives to be 'a negative'. This ranges from genuine criticism to any attempt to talk about feelings or emotions. Instead he's insisted we only talk about 'the positives', meaning we have spoken very little indeed recently. It's very tricky to deal with as he tends to take any suggestion that things aren't going as well as they could as a personal affront. He's sometimes so quick to defend some of the playing squad from critique that I'm starting to wonder if he's their father too.

He's also becoming increasingly obsessed with Neville Peterson and his online feedback. He frequently sends me late-night screenshots of his criticisms, bombarding me with comments from strangers about how badly the team are playing. I've suggested that constantly forwarding these messages doesn't feel like focusing on 'the positives' but Dad maintains this is different. He says it's important to 'keep an eye on your enemies'. I've said that Neville isn't an enemy, he's literally a supporter who just spends too much time online, but this has fallen on deaf ears.

As our first competitive match gets closer we've started to snip and peck at each other. His tone's more blunt and disengaged, mine more passive-aggressive and stroppy. I might be imagining this but I also think he's started to avoid me during matches. We travel to the games together but as soon as they kick off he quickly walks away, circling the ground nomadically, avoiding conversation.

Doing my best to look on the bright side, a recent positive has been that the opening of the outdoor bar was a huge success. In fact it almost doubled our half-time bar takings against Droylsden. An unavoidable negative is that the bar has been closed by the council until further notice after a surprise visit informing us we didn't have the necessary planning permission to build it. We're likely to get approval but we'll need to fill in many forms, then wait and pay a processing fee plus a fine for opening when we shouldn't have, thus cancelling out everything we took on the bar and then some. Dad's not happy about it and has vowed 'not to take it lying down'. He's embarked on a one-man battle against the bureaucracy of the local council and has written several angry emails warning that he'll open the bar without permission. In response, they have threatened to hit us with a further, much higher fine and even the potential forfeiture of our licence to sell alcohol on a match day. I fear he is destined to lose both the battle and any subsequent war.

The truth is, the closer the season gets, the more I find myself fighting against an ever-increasing internal sense of panic. My days are punctuated by bouts of alarm and self-doubt that I do my best to suppress in a game of anxiety whack-a-mole. It's very rare that an hour passes without me worrying about the decisions we're making and their knock-on effects. I often wake up in the night drenched in a cold sweat, asking myself with terror, 'Are we going to be shit?' I lie awake until the early morning worrying about where our goals might come from, when we will get back to winning ways, and if everyone at the club thinks I'm a bit of a knob.

Until a couple of weeks ago I had always assumed every-thing on the pitch would go swimmingly, but in recent weeks I've not been able to shake off the feeling that I may have been naive. That the increased budget won't guarantee success and the team just isn't as good as Jamie and Sandy say it is. That our optimism from a month ago when Angie, Robbo, Deano, Dad and I were watching training together was misplaced.

A huge part of our recruitment strategy (if you can call it that) was a reaction to our meeting with Jamie. We've con-tracted the entire squad to make sure they can't leave if things are going well but I've recently started to realize that we now have the opposite problem: we're unable to get rid of any of our players if things start to go badly. Come what may we are stuck with them, most likely for the rest of the season. Unless of course we're able to transfer them to another club, loan them out or pay them out of their contracts.

We've definitely got a talented team on paper. It's just a shame that we play on grass rather than A4. Watching how some of the lads train and play I'm not sure they really want to be here. It's possible that some of them have been motivated solely by the allure of a guaranteed weekly pay packet that is comparatively higher than other teams in the league. I know that we're paying more than we need to because opposition players have taken great delight in letting me know. I'm hoping this is just mind games.

Larry also seems to know exactly what each player is being paid to the penny. During matches he will appear by my shoulder, seemingly out of nowhere, and comment on what certain players are getting and whether he feels they are earning their keep. He very often feels they are not. I'm not sure where the leak is coming from but I'm pretty sure it's Angie. She will neither confirm nor deny this when asked. Whatever the case, it's becoming clearer by the day that we have taken an almighty gamble and that we really do need to hit the ground running.

Our first season in the BetVictor Northern Premier League looms large and we're as ready as we'll ever be. Despite the damp pre-season, expectations remain high. The general belief among the majority of supporters and volunteers is that we'll be competing to win the league. That once the 'proper football' starts we'll click into gear and find our feet.

After three months of hard graft and even harder lessons, the moment we've been working towards is here. Our first competitive match and inaugural season as joint chairmen. We've rebuilt the squad, built an outdoor bar and partly destroyed our indoor bar. We've changed the changing rooms and hopefully a few hearts and minds in the process. We've started a women's team, albeit one without any players, and even managed to get the club on the local news despite it being a PR disaster. We've met the fans and already had our ups and downs with them, and we've discovered debt that simultaneously nobody and everybody knew about. I've lost half of my savings and an even bigger chunk of my mind. Tony was right. It is a rollercoaster. I just hope I'm not the one who dies!

The start of the season is three days away and only one thing is clear: we are fully committed. Even if we wanted it, there is no way out. Come Saturday, it all begins. Come Saturday, there is nowhere to hide.

There is nowhere to run.

Part Two

7

Kick-off!

I walk down Surrey Street imbued with a sense of purpose, my new tan shoes clacking against the cobbles and a large pair of aviator sunglasses making me look like a bug. It's tremendously hot and the sun shines down on Hurst Cross as the crowd make their way excitedly into the ground. In an hour's time we kick off our season against newly promoted Atherton Collieries. Colls, as they are affectionately known, are playing in the Northern Premier League for the first time in their history. Formed by miners in 1916 in order to raise funds for locals involved in the First World War, they are the bookies' favourite to go down, whereas we're second favourite for promotion. It's a great opportunity to start with a win and hit the grassy ground running.

Supporters gently pour through the turnstiles dressed in shorts and replica shirts. The sense of expectation is palpable. I follow them and listen as they discuss the match and our chances. Some guess the score while others stay tight-lipped as 'Rockin' Robin' by Bobby Day plays over our crackling tannoy system, filling the summer air and adding to the sense of occasion.

There's still half an hour until kick-off so I decide to walk around the ground to greet our supporters and soak up the atmosphere while Dad and the rest of the board entertain visiting directors from the opposition. Which basically means feeding them ham and cheese sandwiches and soup from an urn so large it could cater for an army.

Tom and Bethany are stood with a gaggle of our supporters behind the home dugout. They sip lager and lemonade while fanning themselves with match-day programmes.

'Not a bad turnout for the first day, Mr Chairman,' enthuses Tom.

'Not bad at all,' I reply, shaking his outstretched hand warmly.

Tom's certainly right. We've lucked out today. We're the only local team playing at home in the area which means we've hoovered up a few nomadic non-leaguers. There must be about 400 people here already. If we can put on a good performance hopefully they will choose us as their team for the season or at least come back again.

The Sid Sykes Stand is well populated with players' partners and family members, excited to cheer for their new team, while further down the ground 'The Robin's Nest' tea hut is doing great business. Little Mavis frantically doles out beige food on to polystyrene trays drenched in gravy as more supporters, including Bryan and his husband Ash, join the queue and soak up the sun. Dale's wife Georgina is head chef and loads pies in and out of the oven at record speed.

Our hard-core fans from the supporters' club are behind

the goal at the Rowley Street end. They're already singing 'We're going to win the league', standing in front of a huge red and white flag they've draped on the concrete wall behind the terraces. It reads 'AUFC 4EVA!' An older supporter I've not seen before struggles to summon up enough air to sporadically blow a trumpet while Stella bangs enthusiastically on a marching drum.

'Any thoughts on them free shirts?' she shouts with a grin.

I wave back politely before carrying on towards the Popular Stand, pausing to look out on to the pitch. With the question of how to fill the tank still very much a work in progress, Deano and Dale are doing their best to water the turf using the garden hose running from the bar, but it doesn't quite stretch beyond the halfway line. It means one half of the grass is luscious and green whereas the other looks sun-kissed with hints of hay. Dale runs off down the tunnel and returns with a huge bucket which they fill and carry together towards the driest spots. They bicker sporadically as they work before stopping to give me a quick thumbs up.

My phone buzzes in my pocket. It's Flash. Since our phone call a few weeks ago he's taken to bombarding me with Whats-App videos of new players on a near daily basis. He's letting me know that his new client is the 'best baller he's seen' and that 'we don't want to miss out this time'. I doubt this information on two fronts: firstly that the player is 'the best', and secondly that he's ever seen the player play. I put my phone back in my pocket and my focus back on today.

As I round towards the opposite goal I nod at a few other supporters who greet me merrily, including Phil from the Q&A who's standing next to a furious-looking woman in a

fleece. I wonder if this is the start of some kind of reconcili-
ation and if Phil has moved back into his house? I make my
way up to the directors' lounge and spot Larry and his
podiatrist lover leaning over the terraces, lost in energetic conversation. Larry's dog looks on, waiting, while Frank Taunton,
Neville Peterson and our previous chairman Tony Liverstout
stand a few feet behind, watching on austerely.

'Beautiful Day' by U2 is now blaring over the tannoy and
the ground is filled with a sense of optimism and bonhomie.
Members of the recently formed under-8s and -9s team run
about chasing one another wearing newly printed red 'Little
Robins' tracksuits. They call out to one another and laugh
gleefully as their parents plead with them to stay still, coaxing
them into good behaviour with sweets from the tuck shop.

It's a near perfect atmosphere, and a fantastic advertisement for the non-league game. I climb the stairs of the little
wooden decking area in the corner of the ground, allowing
myself a moment of self-satisfaction. The players are now finishing off their pre-match warm-up and are starting to head
down the tunnel. They joke with one another, and even Jamie
looks relaxed as he talks tactics with Sandy and waves at a
couple of our supporters.

I open the double doors to the directors' lounge. It's an
incredibly unique and narrow space in re-cladded cream that's
partly made from a disused railway carriage, and it also serves
as our boardroom. It has huge double windows looking out
on to the pitch and is filled by a large wooden table and our
trophy cabinet. Or trophy shelf to be more accurate. The
entrance curves out into a little bar area with a couple of
chairs and tables. The walls are adorned with snaps from our

recent play-off-winning team alongside photos from 2013 when we last won the Manchester Cup, and along the back wall are dozens of black and white images of heavily moustached men in even more heavily striped shirts, each wearing a pair of shorts that are almost trouser length. This gallery includes an almost impossibly grainy image of Dixie Dean, who played two games for us just before the Second World War, and an inexplicably youthful shot of Alan Ball, who also played a handful of games for us at the tender age of fifteen. He appeared briefly alongside my grandfather and eventual Liverpool title winner Alf Arrowsmith, both of whom are also members of our small but impressive hall of fame. Other notable names to have pulled on the AUFC jersey include England international and FA Cup finalist Bobby Barclay, Welsh international and top-flight player John Mahoney, and Jamie Hughes, the first British player to be banned for performance-enhancing drugs.

In the middle of the room is a large image of the Lancashire County Combination Trophy winners from 1952, including my grandad. He looks on stoically, his arms folded nonchalantly, with the cup stood respectfully by his feet. I briefly allow myself to wonder if he'd be proud of Dad and me and think what a shame it is that he can't be with us today.

Robbo, Dad and Angie are stood together making small talk with members of the Atherton committee and their guests. They're dressed in brand-new official club blazers and offering our visitors a selection of M&S sandwiches and crisps. They're also joined by our club president Reginald Timpkins, a man who's been at the club longer than anyone else; he was good friends with my grandad and worked with him at British Telecom back in the day. He's a kindly man with neatly combed silver hair and a friendly smile. I make my way over to the group and introduce myself, interrupting a conversation about what an 'unrivalled floodlight system' would look like.

'Good afternoon,' I say, offering my hand. 'Welcome to our club.'

There's an odd pause and our visitors look at me with slight hesitation.

'This is Jonathan,' says Robbo jovially. 'Our chairman.'

Our three guests look at me blankly. One of them, I think her name's Julie, suppresses a smile at the corner of her mouth.

'Oh, right,' she says with performative surprise in her voice.

'You're the club chairman?' asks another with mild incredulity.

'I am,' I reply flatly.

'I thought he was the chairman?' says the other guy.

Robbo explains that we have two co-chairs at the club and that we've both come in as father and son.

'Nice that you're helping your dad out,' Julie adds, somewhat patronizingly.

This is an exchange that I'll get used to as the season goes on. It's frustrating and no doubt pricks at my pride. It also adds to the growing sense of imposter syndrome I'm finding it hard to shake off. I've put a lot of work into the club in the last few months so it's incredibly annoying to forever be fighting the de facto tag of assistant just because I'm younger. A huge part of me wants to shout that joining the club was my idea in the first place and I asked Dad to partner me, but instead I do my best to smile politely.

'We're doing it together,' I respond cordially.

'We're going to have our work cut out today,' states the second guy. 'Especially with all the money we hear you're chucking at it.'

'We try to run our club sustainably,' says Julie.

'Like a proper business,' adds the second guy, twisting the knife.

Dad bristles and I do my best to laugh off the comment, telling them that we too are 'committed to running the club responsibly' while secretly wondering if that's what we're doing. 'We've made a bit of an investment,' I add, 'but don't believe everything you hear on the grapevine.'

'I run a business,' Dad says bluntly, taking the bait hook, line and sinker.

The tannoy bursts into life again, this time to welcome everyone to Hurst Cross. The match is about to start. We head back on to the decking, a small raised wooden platform overlooking the pitch, with a few picnic benches reserved for club directors. The team gathers in the tunnel and a group of our juniors form a guard of honour to welcome them on to the pitch. I get butterflies as Fat Boy Slim's 'Right Here, Right Now' starts to play and the team runs out. They all look impressively focused and are met by rapturous applause.

'We love you Ashton, we do! We love you Ashton, we do!' roar our home supporters from behind the goal, as Stella goes to town on her drum.

'Come on, boys!' bellow Robbo and Angie.

The hairs on the back of my neck stand up and I can feel a surge of adrenalin course through me. I look over to Dad who

I can tell feels the same. He claps his hands with ferocity, nodding in excitement.

'We're actually doing this,' I think to myself.

As the team is read out, the crowd greet each name with a boisterous cheer. There are a couple of surprises on the team sheet. Boothy is fit to start and has been thrown straight into the line-up. It's a bit of a gamble but if he can hit the ground running it will make a huge difference to our season.

The players take their places, jogging on the spot and stretching in anticipation while Jamie, Sandy and the subs make their way to the dugout. They exchange high fives and fist bumps, sharing last-minute words of encouragement with one another. At the halfway line the referee flips a coin and our captain Jono chooses to kick off.

This is it!

Dad and I share a moment of eye contact before oddly making the decision to shake hands. It's not something we've ever done and I doubt we will again.

'Here we go,' I say.

'Break a leg,' Dad responds warmly.

The whistle blows and we're off. We pass the ball about with confidence, zipping it from left to right with attacking intent. Early on we have a few half chances and their keeper is forced to tip the ball over the crossbar after a speculative attempt from 30 yards out. We're having a lot of luck down the right-hand side and the ball fizzes into the box only for Boothy to miss by inches. The crowd will us on vociferously and the mini carnival vibe continues as we probe for an opening. There's a clever one-two down the line prompting some of our fans to burst into spontaneous and slightly ironic song.

'It's just like watching Brazil! It's just like watching Brazil!'

Atherton have the ball but a loose pass sees us regain possession in the middle of the park. Our midfielder Shezza sprays the ball out wide majestically to winger Connor Hughes who miscontrols a little and the ball moves just in front of him. Suddenly one of their players slides in two-footed and totally takes him out. Connor rolls around in pain and the ball goes out of play.

No foul given, and the linesman gives them the throw.

Their manager applauds while Jamie screams fifty shades of blue at the man in black. The crowd jeer with genuine hatred and suddenly the mood around the ground has changed in an instant. Angie is incandescent, Robbo patrols the decking like he's back on the beat, and even gentle Reginald froths with rage. He wrings his hands, calling the opposition every name under the sun, and throws his walking stick to the ground. Larry's dog barks cantankerously, and the beat on the drum from behind the goal now feels less festive and more like a call to war. The air is infected with tribalism, and it will remain this way for the rest of the game.

Eventually play carries on, but not for Connor. His day is done. He hobbles off and heads down the tunnel for a shower as Jamie is forced into an early change.

'Pass and move, boys!' he shouts viciously.

'We keep going, boys!' adds Sandy, clapping encouragingly.

Atherton are starting to press us very hard and for the next ten minutes they put us under constant pressure. We want to play football but there's no space to do it. They suffocate us, rushing us into mistakes all over the pitch. Our plan has gone out of the window and we look full of panic. The ball ricochets around like a pinball as tackles fly in like hungry gulls around a seaside chip shop. Tarantula looks unsettled too, and as the ball is continually pumped forward there are more than a couple of heart-stopping moments as he rushes to collect. When we manage to get our foot on the ball we look threatening, but it feels at times as if Atherton have an extra man. They're striving incredibly hard off the ball, pinning us into our own half and outworking us all over the pitch.

The crowd whistle and boo the opposition with every touch and scream at our own players with hellfire.

'Keep hold of it for fuck's sake!' one fan screams.

'Pass it, you bell-end!' heckles another.

The warmth and joviality of the pre-kick-off mood has melted away, replaced with a hot fire and fury. My hands shake uncontrollably and I can feel my heart pounding out of my chest. When Colls approach our goal I'm terrified they'll score, and when we approach theirs I'm terrified we'll miss.

It's in this moment I have a horrible realization. I hate all of this. I've looked forward to the season starting so much and now all I can think about is how badly I want the game to end. I'm desperate for us to get through it without losing. Every kick of the ball causes me pangs of severe anxiety. All I can do is watch and hope. We hit one wide and I'm robbed of true ecstasy. They hit the bar and I nearly shit myself. It's unbearable, and the only way I can deal with it is to scream obnoxiously at the linesman for catharsis, waving my fists and stomping my feet. I'm an embarrassment. Even Angie is looking at me like I'm overdoing it. Dad's not faring any better. He's puffing his cheeks in and out dramatically. Every time the ball advances past the halfway line in either direction he looks like he's going into labour.

The half-time whistle goes and I'm glad for the respite. The crowd applaud the players as they jog down the tunnel and we take a moment to breathe before heading back into the lounge for a cup of soup and a moment of peace.

I feel a rough tap on my shoulder. I turn round to find Larry and his dog staring at me balefully.

'Disappointing not to break the deadlock yet,' he says with a glimmer in his eyes. 'With what we're spending this season we really should be miles in front.'

I'm flustered and I don't really know what to say so I head in, in search of deliverance from the most intense forty-five minutes of my life. Reginald has reverted to his placid self and is sat drinking a glass of rosé wine, joking about some of our missed chances. Dad, Robbo and Angie are locked in an animated conversation while our guests seem content and comfy.

'Much closer than I thought it would be,' says Julie, greeting me at the entrance with a sly smile.

'It only goes to show you can't buy success,' says the second guy gleefully.

We all congregate together and I prepare myself for fifteen minutes of stilted conversation and Stilton soup. Reginald starts to tell a few stories from the old days while Robbo circles the visiting directors checking if they need refills or additional bread rolls. After five minutes or so Angie heads off to the club office to get a head start sifting through our now bulging payroll. I look out through the window only to be met with a cold glare from Frank Taunton and his septuagenarian gang of ex-directors and former chairmen. They stand in silence looking in at me from the terraces. My buttocks clench as I look out, trying my best to summon up an expression that says 'everything is going to plan', but in truth I most likely look more like a lost child in a supermarket. My heart is still thumping and my head is swirling. Dad, who has been extremely quiet during the break, comes up and begins to unburden himself of his thoughts.

'We should be winning,' he says matter-of-factly.

'It's early days,' I reply defensively.

'These are favourites for relegation,' he fires back.

'Let's just see what happens in the second half. I'm sure we'll improve.'

'I don't get this playing-out-from-the-back crap,' he continues. 'You play football in their half not your own.'

'That's for the manager to decide, not you,' I tell him.

'I'm the chairman!' he snaps back.

'*We're* the chairmen,' I say tempestuously, 'and we're not supposed to interfere with the team.'

'Says who?'

'Everyone,' I reply, getting hot under the collar. 'That's one of the main things everyone says. That the chairman shouldn't get involved with things on the pitch. It's like always on Sky Sports,' I add, sounding like a disgruntled teenager.

'Well I don't like this tippy-tappy, tiki-taka crap. If in doubt, kick it out,' he says, before zipping up his jacket and heading back on to the decking.

I follow him out as the players retake their positions and the second half gets underway. The weather has changed, and so have we. We've gone to three at the back and brought on another winger. It's a clear statement of intent, and once again we start well. We pass the ball around at pace, imposing ourselves from the off.

Then everything changes.

Just a couple of minutes in, the ball is crossed in from deep in the Atherton half. It picks up pace in the air before they head it out for a corner. Shezza runs over to take it. He steadies himself and whips it in. It bends wickedly in the air, flying over everybody's heads, past the keeper and right into the top corner. It's a total fluke but we don't care. We jump about on the decking uncontrollably. I hug Dad and run down to behind our dugout to celebrate with some of our supporters like we've just won the league. Even Phil and his partner jump into each other's arms. Jamie waves his arms aloft and the bench greet the moment with more high fives and fist bumps. The ultras behind the goal are in raptures as they goad the visiting supporters.

'It's all gone quiet over there! It's all gone quiet over there!'

In fairness there are only about twenty Atherton fans here so it's been pretty quiet from the off, but that's beside the point. We're off the mark and I'm enjoying the experience again. I start visualizing a handsome victory and dream of promotion and a season of adventure. I turn to Dad who is beaming ear to ear.

'That's exactly what we needed,' he enthuses. 'Watch, we'll batter them now.'

For a while our sudden confidence seems well placed and as the match continues, the gulf in class between the two sides becomes increasingly evident. We hit the post and have one cleared off the line in the space of ten minutes. A second goal feels inevitable until it all goes wrong. We're caught in possession trying to play out from the back and their striker slots the ball home coolly. Jamie screams at the players as Sandy tries to gee the boys up again. A lead weight hits my stomach and once again I'm on edge. I stand motionless on the decking with my hands cupped over my mouth. Our fans do the same as the Atherton players run to their supporters and celebrate. It's still pretty quiet over there but that doesn't matter. The wind has been taken out of our sails before we were even upstream and we're back to square one.

The complexion of the game completely alters and we're no longer the dominant force. Atherton are growing in confidence and the next ten minutes are end to end. We push forward forcefully but our Cadbury Creme Egg soft centre means we're vulnerable to the counter-attack. We hit the post and nod one just over but they also have their chances. Jono makes a last-ditch tackle that could easily have resulted in a penalty and Tarantula is forced into a smart save at his near post. The emotion of the experience starts to overwhelm me again and I start to google for warning signs of a heart attack.

The minutes tick by and we're still at one apiece with seventy minutes played. The crowd urge us on as we continue to search for a second. The Colls' manager screams at his team to push up as they start to fall deeper. We fire the ball into their box and a scuffed clearance lands at the feet of Shezza. He looks up at goal and drills it right into the bottom corner.

We dance around in jubilation once more, screaming and shouting with abandon. 'Surely we've done enough to win this?' I think to myself. I'd say most people would agree we've been the better team in this half and we've looked confident and composed.

'Concentration is key!' shouts the constantly clapping

Sandy as Colls show their hand and make a couple of substitutions of their own.

The ball's back in the middle of the park and the opposition kick off with just under twenty minutes left on the clock. Any hopes that our guests will roll over and let us coast to our first victory are very quickly put to bed as Atherton start to attack. They go direct, launching the ball deep into our half and pushing forward in numbers. I feel physically sick as the momentum of the game shifts and we try to cling on.

Their manager patrols the touchline, applauding and encouraging.

'We work!' he shouts. 'We keep working!'

As the minutes tick by, they look increasingly tenacious as we appear more and more leggy. What Colls lack in ability they are amply making up for in application and attitude. They're first to every second ball and look totally indefatigable, like a team of Duracell bunnies wired on Red Bull.

Some of our lads are slowing down and others are stopping with cramp. I whisper under my breath, begging for us to hold on, while Dad checks his watch every twenty seconds. The crowd grow quiet and pensive and there are still ten minutes to go.

'Get it up!' shouts Dad forlornly as the ball is wellied back up towards our corner flag.

'We work, we work!' drones their manager on a loop.

Sandy continues to clap and feed in positives while Jamie screams at the lads to keep the ball.

Then disaster strikes. The ball goes out for a goal kick and Tarantula plays it short to Jono who goes to clear but then rolls it across to our left-back. The pass is a little short though, and the number ten for Atherton, who's been a thorn in our side all afternoon, nicks the ball and our defender has no option other than to foul him just outside the area. The ref blows, and although the crowd protest we all know it's the correct call. Their winger Oliver Roberts takes a short run-up and curls the ball right into the top corner past the diving Tarantula. The Atherton players run to their gaffer's dugout and embrace one another, with the goalscorer sliding on his knees, much to Deano's disgust. The home crowd falls silent and we are forced to watch their joy through the mist of our despair. Jamie slams his fist against the dugout in frustration and I bury my head in my hands.

The modest clump of away fans celebrate, and it's their turn to give some stick back to us.

'It's all gone quiet over there!' they sing in unison.

There are only eight minutes left now and I've gone from dreaming of victory to praying we can come away with a point. The crowd shout in exasperation, driving the team forward. We're dead on our feet and out of ideas. They blast the ball wide near the end, and Tarantula makes a solid save to keep them out.

Then, just as the game is fizzling out, one of their players slides in late on our midfielder Tom Forrest. It's totally unnecessary and Tom loses his cool, jumping up and grabbing their player by the scruff of his neck. The rest of the players rush over, and soon everyone is screaming and holding one another back without really knowing what happened. Suddenly it's like the third floor of Debenhams, there's handbags all over the place, and the ref sends both players off. Tom pulls his shirt over his head despondently while their player gives a little smile to their manager as he departs. We all endure three minutes of uneventful added time before the final whistle blows and the match comes to a conclusion.

The Hurst Cross faithful disperse and slowly start to make their way to the bar while the players from both teams shake hands and share a few words. Atherton certainly look more pleased than we do and they wander over to their gaggle of supporters to thank them for making the short trip from the borough of Wigan. Our players disappear rapidly, no doubt ready to receive a roasting from Jamie. We've not been awful but we've certainly not been good. It's been a patchy match. We've played the better football but we've been outworked by an opposition who just wanted it more than us.

I lean forward over the balcony, absolutely exhausted. I'm utterly drained and my legs feel like they could give way. It's been end to end and full of incident and I've despised every moment of it, except maybe the few seconds of relief after our goals. It's been painful, stressful and, to be honest, a little scary, and the whole experience makes me wonder if I will ever be able to enjoy football again. There are twenty-two teams in our league plus cup games, so that means a minimum of forty-three games left to go. That's another 3,870 minutes exactly to endure – over sixty-four hours. Plus all the added time.

I look out and watch our volunteers who are already busying themselves around the ground. The media team conduct their post-match with Jamie, while Robbo and Reginald wish our visiting directors well, sending them on their way with yet more lukewarm soup and a stash of sandwiches for the drive home. Angie scurries about to make sure the players are paid while Mavis and Georgina ensure there are hot pies and peas ready for them too. Deano and Dale have quietly begun repairing the divots on the pitch in preparation for next time. I'm suddenly filled with admiration for each and every one of them. Some of them have been here for over fifteen years and hardly ever miss a game. Reginald is now in his fifty-fourth season at the club! They are either all made of stronger stuff than me or they're masochists.

Dad heads into the bar for a few drinks to calm his near shredded nerves. I stay outside and allow my mind to drift as the ground slowly empties and the sun begins to dip in the late-afternoon amber sky.

Newly washed shirts are laid out over the ad boards to dry while litter is picked from the terraces. Highlights are clipped and cut together for social media and empty barrels bereft of beer are rolled noisily on to the pavement. Hours drift by as a cool breeze whispers through Hurst Cross. I shiver a little as the work on the field continues and the afternoon gives way to the evening.

It really hits me in this moment just how much dedication goes into keeping the club running. The quiet industry that is poured into the place by our volunteers. Their often unnoticed efforts fuelled by love for their club and community. I see the dejection that the failure to win is met with and it suddenly dawns on me the weight of the responsibility we have taken on. A draw feels gutting; imagine what it's going to be like when we lose! I must make sure their endeavour is rewarded in the way it deserves to be. I can't let them down. This *has* to work.

One by one they depart and the hum from the bar starts to

fade, and finally the floodlights flicker off and the stadium is closed for the night. The bell for last orders rings faintly in the distance and the cheering and chatter come to a halt. There's silence, and for the first time today all is calm. My heart rate returns to normal, the remaining adrenalin drips out of my body, and I am able to breathe.

'Shit,' I think to myself. 'I'm locked in the ground.'

8

Don't Count Your Chickens

My arrival at the Sir Tom Finney Stadium marks the end of a six-and-a-half-hour journey from London to Bamber, a former textile village three miles south-east of Preston. I'm here to watch our match against Bamber Bridge FC. It's our third league game of the season after a 3–0 weeknight loss away at South Shields.

As I head towards the turnstile I'm greeted by Deano who says he needs to talk to me about the new TV screen in the changing room. Apparently it doesn't work and Jamie isn't very happy about it. Depressingly, the reason seems to be the complete absence of any electrical wiring. We've been ripped off by the builder.

'As far as I can tell it's purely aesthetic,' says Deano wearily. 'We'd have to break through the wall to get to the back of the TV.'

'I think you're best speaking to my dad about it,' I sigh.

'Yeah I thought that too but I couldn't get through to him this week. We tend to go to him for anything that's practical or football-related.'

I scream inwardly.

'What do you come to me for then?' I ask Deano.

'The other stuff,' he replies cagily.

'Like what?' I say.

'Just anything that's not a problem or about football,' he responds.

'Right, from now on, Deano, any practical issue comes straight to me,' I snap.

'But how will it get sorted?' he asks.

I promise him it will and head into the ground, keen to protect what's left of my ego.

Despite our most recent result, morale remains pretty high among supporters. South Shields are the only professional club in the division so losing there is certainly no disgrace. It's also a hell of a journey for a Tuesday night and we ended up with several members of the squad unable to play due to not being able to get the time off work and a minimal following of six away supporters to cheer us on. I also wasn't able to make it and was forced to settle for following the match via our Twitter page.

Today we're in a better position. We have a contingent of forty-six supporters here, and Jamie has a full squad to pick from. He's told me that on Thursday we trained well using a new 3-5-2 system, and he's expecting us to take home three points. After last Saturday I'm determined to keep my emotions in check and try to enjoy the experience a little. It's a quintessential non-league ground, with a convivial atmosphere and lush greenery on all sides. There's a huge rust-speckled stand on one sideline and on the other the terraces fold up into grassy mounds with houses and trees behind. There's an enormous clubhouse, with a bar and a pair of doors that open out on to the pitch where a row of picnic benches have been carefully positioned for the perfect match-day experience. Kick-off is still half an hour away so I decide to have a half pint to help me relax.

I've been thinking all week about how we can make sure our work off the pitch translates to what's happening on it. After the dispiriting Tuesday defeat I started to consult Google on how I can play my part and influence what is going on from the sidelines. The closest thing to an answer I've found so far is to 'manifest' our success. In short, to know what you want and to think it until it comes to fruition. I figure if it's good enough for Oprah and Noel Edmonds it's good enough for me and Ashton United. So on my train journey up I have followed the guidance of lawsofattraction.com to the letter. I've written down what I desire most deeply, in this case a win. I've asked the universe to make it so, and I have removed any mental barriers that might get in the way, mainly the idea that this is nonsense and I'm grasping at straws. In short, I will maintain belief in our victory no matter what. I will be the Ted Lasso that AUFC needs!

I wander over to the clubhouse ready to chat to some of our fans and to spread the news that today's result is in the bag, as long as we all remain positive. The first people I come across are Bethany and her dad Tom.

'Hiya, Jonathan,' Bethany chimes, a couple of dark fruit ciders in. 'Ready for the match?'

'Ready for the three points?' I ask as matter-of-factly as possible.

'You sound confident,' Tom replies in good cheer.

'I always am,' I say brightly. 'We just need to believe in the team,' I add, as if I have just imparted a great secret of life.

'Righto,' responds Tom without much thought as they both head off to pick their spot for the first half.

I stand in the middle of the bar doing my best to exude positivity. Smiling at those I know, hoping to inspire and, most importantly, attract the elusive win. I meditate serenely on the thought of goals but I'm interrupted when a home fan knocks into me carrying several pints, tipping half the contents down my shirt.

'Move!' he shouts. 'Why are you just standing in the thoroughfare like that?'

I apologize and decide to manifest in the queue, where I am out of the way and able to get a drink. Once I've done this I take my place behind the goal and run into Dad, who's just arrived.

'Nervous?' he asks, looking nervous.

'Not at all, the win is guaranteed,' I say with a forced confidence.

Dad shoots me a strange look but doesn't bite.

'Hope you've not bribed the officials,' booms Robbo, appearing behind us with his family in tow.

There's a little laughter from the supporters around us as we ready ourselves for the game. Music blasts from the tannoy and the teams run out. I close my eyes to try to visualize free-flowing football and a scoreboard showing a 3–0 victory in our favour.

'I think we're going to win,' I shout to nobody in particular.

We start the game very well, testing their keeper early doors. The change in formation suits us and we overload them in the middle of the park. Our movement is fantastic and we seem really up for the game. It's more enjoyable being surrounded by the supporters than stood alone on the decking and I'm able to watch the game without worrying as much. After fifteen minutes a long-distance effort from Boothy hits the bar, before he narrowly nods one wide. We certainly look confident and it's no surprise when we take the lead after thirty-eight minutes, our versatile defender/midfielder/striker Josh Wilson heading in from a beautifully placed cross by the always reliable Shezza. We're untroubled for the rest of the half and I continue to build a mental picture of the journey back to London with three points in the bag.

'Much better than Tuesday,' Dad says, impressed with our first-half performance.

'I believe,' I say firmly.

He ignores me and continues talking. Although he's happier with how we're playing today he's concerned we've not taken enough of our chances and we should be more than one goal to the good. 'You don't get points for creating chances, you get them from taking them,' he adds with all the wisdom of a fortune cookie.

Robbo seems pretty chuffed, as does Angie, who promises me a lift to the train station after the match. She's joined today by Larry who she's driven from the club.

'We're pretty good today aren't we, Larry?' I say as effusively as possible, hoping to sweep him up in my positivity.

'One thing I've learnt from my time in the game is that a match can change in an instant,' he warns sternly. 'It's a fool who counts his chickens or his victories at half-time, young Jonathan.'

Determined not to be dragged down I dodge the pessimism like Neo evading bullets and assure him that today will be our day. 'We've just got to keep believing. The three points will be ours,' I conclude, explaining that I have manifested the win for us today.

'Sounds like a load of old tripe to me,' he replies before heading off in search of a half-time cheeseburger.

The match resumes, and it's immediately clear that whatever has been said at half-time hasn't worked. We're less settled and there's a tentativeness to our play. I can feel my stomach starting to churn but try to ignore it and remain positive. I call out affirmations whenever something doesn't go our way and stand with my chest puffed out, hoping my body language will rub off on the players. Bamber hit the post and I shout 'We have faith in you!' at the top of my lungs. We make an error and I scream 'You're all fantastic!' I get the feeling that this isn't necessarily having the inspiring effect I'm aiming for when I spot a couple of the Bamber players laughing and our captain looking at me with disdain. I decide to continue to manifest in a less embarrassing way.

Just as we start to string a few passes together we lose the ball inside our own half and the scores are level. Danny Forbes is played through on goal and makes no mistake as he slots home coolly through Tarantula's legs. I feel my heart beating but I'm determined not to fall into the pit of panic. I keep imagining the team looking composed and try to hold on to the certainty I had earlier that we would be victorious.

'Come on, boys!' I cry, doing my best to revive the spirits of my fellow Robins fans.

It's not looking good though, and the players all seem

rattled. Bamber are having a lot of joy down the right-hand side and our defender and full-time Uber driver Kyle Harrison is having a torrid time. He's beaten again by their speedy winger and we're only saved from going 2–1 down by some awful finishing from their striker. Kyle knows he's having a shocker, not just because he's let another cross into the box but because Jamie wastes no time in telling him from the dugout. Eventually he's hauled off and fans' favourite Aaron Chalmers is brought on to replace him. Aaron is a real character. He's been at the club for four years and was our captain last season. He recently lost the armband to Jono though and fell out with Jamie at training a couple of weeks ago. The crowd greet our substitute warmly and Aaron gives us a thumbs up as he takes his position on the pitch.

Our goalscorer Josh drops back into midfield and we revert to four at the back with Boothy up top on his own. A sign that Jamie might be happy to settle for a point.

It's all getting pretty tense and the hosts are rarely out of our half. Their crowd are growing in confidence and volume whereas we've all fallen into an anxious hush. We're on the ropes and it feels like all we can do is hope that Bamber's level drops.

Then, totally against the run of play, we pump the ball upfield and there's some kind of mix-up in their defence resulting in a full-on goalmouth scramble. It all happens so quickly but the ball falls to Chalmers who manages to toe-poke it in and restore our lead. The opposition look crestfallen as our players celebrate. Dad smiles with satisfaction, Angie dances with glee, and the rest of our travelling faithful are jubilant. Even Larry punches the air victoriously as the goalscorer is announced to a near silent stadium. There's less than twenty minutes left on the clock and it looks like we're going to nick a win.

It works! Manifestation works! I feel lighter than air. It's going to be OK! We've got a great team, we've got a manager who knows how to get promoted from this league, we're building a long-term plan, and I've mastered the art of manifesting in a matter of days!

'I told you we were going to win,' I say to Dad, beaming ear to ear, allowing myself to fully savour the moment.

'Get in!' shouts Dad in an outpouring of emotion.

The next few minutes are a joy to watch. We move the ball with precision and accuracy, building out from the back with a sense of ease as the clock counts down. The minutes fly by until there are just five remaining. There are even a few shouts of 'Olé!' as the Bamber players struggle to get hold of the ball.

Dad scrolls through his phone and looks at the league tables as they stand.

'This puts us sixth,' he says, pushing his screen in front of me.

It's really not bad considering we've not performed at our best yet.

There's a fantastic one-two and Shezza strikes the ball beautifully, rattling the bar.

The soufflé of ever-rising euphoria is sunk on eighty-seven minutes when Bamber win a corner. Tarantula comes out confidently to claim the cross but he gets nowhere near it and is beaten to it by Bridge talisman Gary Pett, who thunders a header into our goal. We all fall noiseless again as the footballing rollercoaster plummets us back down to earth. My gut twists and I feel the first full wave of anxiety surging through me. The lads look utterly shellshocked, and as we kick off the home crowd are now vociferous in their support and, like hungry predators, smelling blood.

I stick to my guns and believe as hard as I can. 'There's still time!' I hear myself shouting in an alarmed voice as Dad reels off a list of the many things we could have done to avoid conceding the corner in the first place.

'Just boot it forward!' he hollers, red-faced. 'They can't score if it's in their half!'

Little Mavis looks devastated and solemnly starts to remove her club apron for the journey home. Angie waves her arms around uselessly, as Stella bangs the drum with even more force.

'Give it a rest!' shouts Robbo in tired frustration.

'Keep your hair on,' retorts Bryan's husband Ash.

The crowd jeer in appreciation as Robbo storms off to watch what's left of the game from another part of the ground, the fading sun reflecting off the top of his head.

'We still need that goalscorer,' shouts Bryan in my direction. 'Boothy still hasn't got one.'

'We must be patient,' I reply vacuously, sounding like a pound-shop Obi-Wan Kenobi.

We focus on the last few minutes of the match and I start coming up with ways to spin the draw as a positive, fielding questions in a press conference that's taking place exclusively in my head. 'Are you up to the job?' 'Two points out of nine is pretty awful, isn't it?' 'You're letting everyone down. What are you going to do about it?'

There's no time to answer any of these questions though.

On ninety minutes exactly Bamber spill forward in numbers. The ball is laid off to one of their midfielders, who rifles it into the corner of the net from 35 yards out. It's a magnificent finish and a painful sucker punch for all of us. Angie puts her head in her hands and Dad goes ballistic, kicking the shit out of the metal fence at the front of the pitch to the point where he's told to stop by one of their stewards. I stand behind our supporters, rooted to the spot, feeling like my insides have been scooped out like cheap school ice cream. We remain in our places for another two minutes, totally numb, until the final whistle blows and brings the match to a close. Bamber Bridge 3 Ashton United 2. We've lost again. It's officially a terrible start to the season. In the first three games we've conceded eight, scored only four, and have just a single point on the board.

The players traipse off disconsolately and Jamie legs it down the tunnel ready to give them a roasting. The kitmen empty our bottles of water on to the pitch forlornly from the dugout as they begin their post-match duties. Dale fills in some forms pitchside as the home fans serenade us.

'Cashton, Cashton, they've tried to buy the league and they've won fuck all!'

'Never count your chickens, young Jonathan,' says Larry sternly as he heads off with Angie to her car.

9

The Boardroom

It's the morning after the night before and we're gathered in the boardroom for a crisis meeting. Things have gone from bad to worse and we're now five league games in and still without a win. If you include our pre-season games it's now over two months since our last victory.

Everybody looks tired and miserable. Robbo is ashen-faced and Angie is downright despondent and has confided in me that she no longer looks forward to our matches which were the highlight of her week. Deano is hung-over and cross that I've replaced the kettle with a fancy coffee machine. Dad is quiet and morose. He sits back in his chair constantly staring at and refreshing the league table on his phone, willing it to change. The room is silent other than the pitter-patter of the rain falling lightly on the roof. The framed photos dotted about the room of moustached men holding aloft trophies look down on us mockingly. I find it hard to meet my grandfather's likeness in the eye.

Our loss to Bamber Bridge was swiftly followed by a truly woeful display at home against local rivals Stalybridge Celtic, where we were lucky to lose 2–0. We were then held to a 1–1 draw against second-in-the-league Matlock. Given our form it would have been a creditable result. However, after the final whistle, I was immediately told by Angie that we had failed to properly register our promising new winger Niall Somerset, meaning we'll be penalized for fielding an ineligible player. We're not sure exactly what mistake we've made but clearly an important piece of paperwork has been missed, lost or forgotten. The punishment is likely to range from a one- to a three-point deduction. This means, best-case scenario, we'll have one point out of a possible fifteen, and worst-case, minus one point, leaving us rooted to the bottom of the table. Niall is now fully registered but is unlikely to play for us again as it's come to light that just before signing for us he pleaded guilty to driving without a licence, fleeing the police and resisting arrest. It's apparently almost certain he'll receive a custodial sentence.

I feel utterly dreadful. I just don't understand why things aren't working. My days are becoming punctuated by a voice that pops up in my head to remind me that I am failing, letting everyone in the town down, and it's only a matter of time before they all realize how clueless I am, if they haven't realized already. At our last match I had a full-on panic attack and was forced to hide behind the industrial-size bins at the back of the Sid Sykes Stand to avoid being seen.

I'm hugely regretting my claim that people should come to me to solve practical problems. I am deeply impractical and have no idea how to fix any of the issues that are rapidly coming my way.

I have a long and ever-growing to-do list of stuff that I'm

currently not doing and wouldn't know how to do even if I tried. Which I have. The list includes a broken pump in the bar, a smashed window, a blocked kitchen sink, damp in the away changing room, broken seats in the stand, intermittent electricity in the tea hut and, of course, the TV in the changing room.

To compound all of this I have trapped a nerve in my neck from over-celebrating our single goal, meaning I'm unable to move my head without experiencing excruciating pain.

I've also begun to genuinely fear the post-match criticism of Neville Peterson, the unanonymous AnonymousRobin, whose incessant online rancour is almost inescapable. Especially as Dad insists on screenshotting and sending me most of his Facebook posts despite my pleas for him not to. Neville paints a picture of a club in turmoil, turgid football on the pitch and confusion behind the scenes. I'm starting to worry that he could be right.

Although the majority of our fan base remain supportive of Dad and me, I'm starting to notice a growing level of criticism directed towards our manager Jamie. His case hasn't been helped by his decision to drop fans' favourite Aaron Chalmers and fine him for a series of indiscretions. Last night there was a tweet in response to our match report reading 'time for change' that garnered four likes. Deano is shaken by it and says we have a potential revolt on our hands, whereas Dad says it's most likely a Russian bot. Nobody knows who @A56UTDB is.

Also on the alarming agenda today: the council have informed us that the concrete enclosure around the pitch where our advertisement boards go is not compliant with health and safety regulations and needs to be replaced as soon as possible. Moreover, the league ground grading officer has told us we must carry out significant works to our outdoor toilets before the season is over, and the hygiene officer is coming to visit to inspect our tea hut. On top of this we're still waiting for planning permission to build the outdoor bar we've already built. We've been told this could still take several months.

In brighter news, our women's team have played their first friendly match. In less bright news they lost 21–0 to Fleetwood Wrens. To be fair, Fleetwood play several leagues above us and our league form since then has been better. We've managed to lose by much lower scorelines.

After a few more minutes of subdued silence, Dad slams his phone down on the table, interrupting the gloomy silence. 'Shall we get going?' he says abruptly. Taking charge of the meeting that I've called. 'Let's talk about the results.'

'We'll go through my agenda,' I say, trying to be assertive while also trying to keep my head as still as humanly possible.

Dad blows out his cheeks in frustration and crosses his arms with the energy of a child who's just been told they can't have sweets before dinner. As the results have declined we've both grown tetchy with each other and our communication has become increasingly terse. He's more remote and uncompromising, and I'm more irritated by his remoteness and inability to compromise.

We've had several arguments. He refuses to use email, meaning I'm often blindsided by events and decisions that have been made without my knowledge. This includes giving the green light to bring in several new players, agreeing to pay one player out of his contract just to get rid of him, and the inexplicable purchase of extra kit. We've burnt through a chunk of money we thought we'd have in reserve and we're going to have to put more cash into the club in December to keep the books balanced. Dad's opinion is that what we are doing isn't working and action is needed. Mine is that we need to be resolute and let the team bed in. At present the starting eleven is changing more than a traffic light running on fast forward.

He's relentless in his view that we need to play simpler football and bangs on about it all the time. He calls me on the phone non-stop to explain that we don't have the technical ability to play with the 'total football' philosophy Jamie is intent on implementing. After the Bamber match he and Jamie got into a row about our playing style, with the latter insisting that the game had moved on and that results wouldn't improve if we just started hoofing the ball forward. The former pointed out that we had conceded a lot of stupid goals we didn't need to. I ended up mediating and not giving my opinion at all, and then being annoyed at myself later for being ineffective.

Dad also complains about the number of WhatsApp groups we have (eleven and counting), which he says is 'ridiculous' and 'overly bureaucratic'. Secretly I know he's right, but I won't admit it. Instead I've doubled down and created a new WhatsApp group just to spite him. This group is simply called 'Club Meetings' and is to be used for – you've guessed it – booking in meetings. There have been countless requests to meet over the next few weeks about trivial things that will eat up our time. I know this is my fault but I've backed myself into a corner where I am forced to pretend that all these conclaves are vital. So we now have in the diary a meeting about grass seed, a meeting about the pool table in the bar, and a meeting about whether goats should be allowed on the pitch for a community event with a petting zoo.

'The first thing to discuss is our recent results,' I say unsurely.

'That's what I just said,' protests Dad.

'Yes, but I'm going through the agenda,' I reply with the charm of a stroppy teenager as a pain shoots sharply up my nape.

'Handbags, ladies,' warns Angie unhelpfully.

We begin, and the board unanimously agree that the results have been very bad. We agree that the team is better than our league table suggests and although we've not played well enough we've also been unlucky. We've had several penalties given against us that weren't penalties, goals given that were blatantly offside, and we've had a huge amount of misfortune in front of goal, with shots being cleared off the line, goalkeepers turning in inspired performances and the woodwork becoming the star of the show in many of our fixtures. We also agree that we are looking at this objectively and with no hint of bias. The thing that is proving more difficult to agree on is what we can do to improve our fortunes.

'It's very early days,' booms Robbo with his usual confidence. 'The worm will turn!'

'Absolutely,' chimes Angie, doing her best to smile. 'Once we get that first win everything will change.'

Dad looks consoled by this take on things. I nod hungrily. Perhaps there is no need for alarm. Maybe we're getting all our season's bad luck in one hard-to-digest meal and we just need to ride the storm out and wait for everything to click into place. After all, Jamie has got us promoted from this league before and knows what he's talking about.

I look across the table at Deano for further reassurance but he appears much more straight-faced about the whole thing. It could be his hangover but he's wearing a sullen expression and gently shakes his head.

'He's lost the dressing room,' he says bluntly. 'He did last season and he has again.'

'It's possible,' says Robbo, making an immediate U-turn.

'I was out with Aaron Chalmers last night and he says we need to get rid,' says Deano.

'He would say that though,' counters Angie. 'I've got a better chance of making the starting eleven than him.'

'I know Jamie has done a lot, Ange,' Deano continues as he rubs his temples, 'but every dog has its day. Just look at my old Alsatian. The club are spending good money and it's some of the worst football I've seen at Hurst Cross. We all saw that tweet. It's going viral.'

We bat the issue back and forth. I feel torn. On the one hand I know that we're in a predicament and strong, decisive action early on in the season could be just what we need to turn the corner, but on the other hand I'm not 'strong and decisive'. We'd also be sacking one of the most successful managers in our recent history. Jamie got us promoted and got us to the play-offs before that. If we need to make a change, who would we even change to, and would they do any better? Plus, I really don't want to fire him. Jamie is a nice bloke. He's a bit scary sometimes but he's a decent guy who's trying his best. Sacking people is really not something I'm sure I have the stomach for. It goes against the people-pleasing part of me that runs through my core. Besides, I've always been super-critical of Premier League clubs who get rid of their manager as soon as things aren't going their way.

We rake over each of our forgettable fixtures in detail and discuss each match blow by blow. What happened, what didn't happen, and where the blame might lie. We also look desperately for evidence that our luck is about to change and better days are around the corner.

We've got a huge weekend coming up that we need to be a success. It's our first qualifying match of the FA Cup and it's a chance to press the reset button and claw back some of the feel-good factor from the start of the season that's so badly ebbed away. We've been drawn away against Tadcaster Albion who ply their trade in the BetVictor Northern Premier League East Division, one league below us. When the draw came out early in the season we were all delighted, but considering how we've been playing we're now worried about this being a potential banana skin of a game.

It's at this point Deano makes a fatal error. He tries to tell Dad what to do. This never works and always has the opposite effect. It didn't work when the doctor suggested he cut down on red meat, it didn't work when I suggested he wore his sun hat on holiday, and it isn't going to work now.

'You need to act,' Deano says. 'He's got to go.'

Dad puffs his chest out as his nostrils flare indignantly. He sits up tall in his seat, resting clenched fists on the table.

'He won't be going anywhere, Deano,' Dad responds firmly. 'Jonathan and myself have faith, *total* faith, in the manager.'

'How can you? We're second bottom and spending a

fortune!' Deano's on the attack, bubbling with frustration and last night's lager.

'Let me worry about that,' Dad says with a sense of finality, itching to slam the brakes on the conversation.

'Let's not fall out,' I intervene tepidly, looking straight ahead, unable to turn towards either of them.

'We've got players claiming they're injured when they're not because they don't want to play for him,' Deano protests.

'Well they have to,' thunders Robbo, suddenly incredibly animated, his patience for players acting with independence let alone disrespect for the club always wafer thin. 'Players these days are a disgrace. Have you seen the state of their socks?'

'Come on everyone,' I say, falling into my usual role of peacekeeper without opinion. My aversion to conflict is so pronounced that I can't take the slightest disagreement without feeling heart palpitations. 'We all want the same thing, and that includes Jamie. To sort this mess out and start moving up the table. I think Angie is right; we get our first win and every-thing turns. So let's keep calm and carry on.'

At that point a car engine backfires outside and I scream out loud, turning my head abruptly as I duck for cover, adding insult to injury.

The meeting continues, but there's now an added tension in the room, and even more tension in my neck and spine.

We move on to the next point on the agenda – attendance figures. When we arrived we promised to slowly increase crowd numbers at the club, but if anything the number of those attending on a match day is in decline. After the defeat to Staly-bridge there was a drop in our gate of over sixty.

'People voting with their feet,' Deano asserts, clearly still agitated.

'Don't be daft,' interjects Robbo dismissively, rolling up the sleeves of his blue check shirt. 'Bridge is a derby; there's always a bigger crowd.'

'There could be an exodus from the club. I've not seen Harold Potes all season,' Deano responds forebodingly.

'That's because he died two years ago,' snaps Robbo.

'I'm just saying, people are unhappy and doing nothing isn't going to change anything.'

'We've done loads,' Dad snaps. 'We're just not doing what you want, Deano.'

It's true, we have done a lot in a short space of time. I'm starting to realize we've probably made a lot of mistakes but we certainly can't be accused of inactivity. In the space of a few short months we've made huge improvements to the ground and the social club, brought in thousands of pounds' worth of investment and sponsorship and set up a variety of new teams. The problem is, all of this counts for nothing if the men's first team are losing every week.

'Let's keep to the agenda,' I plead as the pain in my neck builds.

I feel exhausted. I've been driving or taking the train to and from my home in London for matches and meetings since pre-season, so I've been doing at least 500 miles a week and I can feel it catching up with me. I desperately need a little momentum to help carry us along. At the moment every day feels like starting from scratch again and it's becoming an uphill battle.

'Deano, we'll monitor the results of course,' I concede,

hoping to get him back onside. 'Changing the manager five games in feels reactionary to me.'

'That's the point,' he says. 'To react.'

'Let's just move on for now, my love,' says Angie firmly.

Deano's not happy but he acquiesces with a gruff nod and we move on. Angie's keen to talk about Dale, who she's concerned about. He's been taking on more and more jobs at the club and she fears he's at breaking point. He's recently been diagnosed with retinopathy and has been signed off work until he gets an op. He says it's an overreaction and that his eyes are fine, but yesterday he crashed the mower through the advertising boards because he didn't see them. Fortunately for us we needed to remove them by the end of the season anyway, but it's worrying. She's mindful of hurting his pride if we have to find someone else to take over for a bit.

'He loves that mower,' Angie says, full of compassion, 'but we need to make sure he doesn't hurt himself.'

'Or someone else,' adds Robbo. 'What if there was a dog or a baby on the pitch?'

'Why would there be a baby on the pitch?' Deano asks.

'Well there shouldn't be, obviously,' Robbo says. 'It's most likely against league protocol for starters. I'm just saying, we have to be careful.'

'Especially if we go ahead with the goat for the community event,' counsels Angie.

The matter is discussed for far too long and in the end we agree to do very little: to monitor the situation and to make sure nobody brings small dogs or newborns on to the pitch when the grass is being cut. We've now been going for nearly four hours and we're moving through each point very slowly without making many decisions.

Dad is clearly getting frustrated by the whole thing. He's broken into a sweat and keeps glancing at the clock. Everyone else looks pretty browbeaten too. I move us on to our next point – communication, customized email addresses and WhatsApp groups – and Dad can take no more. He taps the table with his knuckles and says that he needs to leave as he has 'proper stuff to do for the morning'. This cues an actual mass exodus and pretty soon everyone is making excuses and making a move. Angie has grandchildren coming over, Robbo has dinner plans, and Deano 'needs to sleep off' his headache. In fairness I also need to start making the long journey back. Coats are put on, chairs are stacked and mugs of cold tea dispensed into the sink.

'See you all at Tadcaster,' shouts Robbo as he makes his way to the door.

'Absolutely, Mr Roberts,' says Angie with as much cheer as she can muster. 'We'll get that win and everything will fall into place, you'll see.'

'I do hope so,' adds Deano with sincerity, gathering his bag to join Dale on the pitch.

'See you soon,' Dad says to everyone as he follows Robbo out of the door and to his car.

And with that the meeting is over. Everyone is gone. It's just me and the photographs of successful times gone by.

Six days until we play Tadcaster.

A game we simply cannot lose.

10

Green Shoots

It has at last been a decent few weeks at the club and the foot-balling rollercoaster is finally, albeit shakily, on the ascent. I'm quietly hoping that things might at last be clicking into place as I arrive at Hurst Cross for a midweek fixture against Whitby Town.

After a fortuitous draw against Tadcaster, we eventually managed to get our first competitive victory of the season, winning the replay at Hurst Cross by four goals to two. We then followed it up with our first league win at Mickleover where we ran out 1–0 winners before repeating the scoreline against a physical Pontefract Collieries side to book our spot in the next round of the FA Cup qualifiers. Our uplift in form has come at the exact same time Boothy has rediscovered his goalscoring prowess, having bagged three goals in four games, and the arrival of reliable goalkeeper Dave Carnell. Our women's team has also started to pick up some creditable results, and for a side entirely assembled only two months ago we're proudly sitting lower mid-table.

Sadly I've not been around to see any of these improvements

because of work, and it's been suggested by some that perhaps I'm unlucky and should stay away from the club until the end of the season. I feel this is a little unfair given that we were absolutely rubbish last season and I was never there.

The income gained from our mini FA Cup run means the club will lose less money than it normally does. When I say the club I of course mean me and Dad, who are guaranteeing the club's coffers against the losses for the season. Until now these losses have been large and consistent. I'm due to get married in a few weeks' time and I'm scared my commitments to the club are going to force us to downsize the scale of the ceremony. I have already asked my soon-to-be wife how she would feel if we disinvited some of her family and relocated the ceremony to the living room. She's not given me an answer yet.

The truth is, our shocking start to the season has left us walking a proverbial tightrope where we are perpetually only two bad results away from a crisis. It's left me the captive of a constant and creeping sense of dread. I'd hoped that after our first win I might start to enjoy myself, but the dopamine hit and relief were short-lived and it didn't take long for me to start fretting about the next match.

In fact my weeks have started to take on a very similar shape. I start worrying about the weekend on Thursday evening and become increasingly fearful on Friday. I spend Saturday full of nerves and I'm usually disconsolate on Sunday. I panic all day Monday about our midweek fixture, on Tuesday I'm wrapped in fear, and no matter the result I'm ruined by Wednesday. I've worked out that the only time my heart rate is anywhere near restful is the first half of Thursday. It's a weekly routine that has left my nervous system in tatters, and I genuinely think the opening of the season might have given me a low-level form of PTSD.

Whitby are high-flying so far. They're third in the league and joint top scorers. Everybody knows we're going to have our work cut out but there's a real belief that we may have turned a corner. For a Tuesday night we have a decent attendance of almost 200, and with the Whitby squad having had to travel over 120 miles on a school night to get here there's a quiet but unspoken feeling among the Hurst Cross faithful that we could, and probably should, get something from tonight's game.

Dad has blocked several volunteers from writing in the match-day programme, deeming their contribution to be too critical. I've told him he is behaving like an authoritarian government, which he's taken as a compliment. Short on reading material for tonight's supporters, the programme now features a very vague article I've cobbled together about 'unity' and 'birds flying together'. It's without doubt one of the worst things I've ever written in my life. It ends with the sentence: 'Birds of a feather must flock together and so let us fly up the league table as one.' I'm just pleased that only about twelve people buy the programme and even fewer actually read it.

It's crisp and cold and the grass is gloriously illuminated by the floodlights. Like a congregation arriving at church, everyone has taken to their usual pew ready for the ninety-minute service to begin. I'm stood on the decking still wearing my slightly too big coat. In my pocket, acting as a makeshift lucky rabbit's foot, is the programme Dad gave me all those years ago when I first saw us play against Ossett Albion. It was only when I arrived at the ground and showed it to one of our

supporters that I was reminded the team lost 3–1 so it's probably more of a bad omen than a lucky charm. I briefly wonder
if it's the programme that's been the cause of our bad luck so
far. This includes a recent injury crisis that means we are
unlikely to be able to name a full bench of five this evening.

Thankfully there's no time to dwell on any of this as the
team run out ready to begin. The crowd cheer warmly and I
feel my heartbeat increase as I start to pray to a God who until
this season I never knew I believed in.

Jamie has named an incredibly offensive line-up, with five
attack-minded players starting plus our midfield maestro
Shezza in the centre. Aaron Chalmers has been dropped
entirely, and our new keeper Dave Carnell has retained his
place. Tarantula is on the bench. So too is an unusually nega-
tive-looking Sandy who has taken one for the team and joined
the squad for the evening to make sure we have defensive cover
among the substitutes. I sidle up to the dugout and ask him
how he feels about potentially getting some minutes on the
pitch.

'Break glass only in case of massive fucking emergency,' he
says grimly.

Jamie smiles and applauds the lads from his technical area
as they finish stretching. He looks like he's enjoying being the
laid-back member of the double act for a change.

The match gets underway, and we start brightly and full of
purpose. We've been here before though so I don't allow
myself to relax in any way. I remain hyper-vigilant and impossibly tense, keen to avoid any potential heartbreak. We advance
on their goal and I do everything I can to keep myself on an
even keel. We rattle the bar early on and I stare out impassively;

their keeper denies us with a flying save and I remain as stoic as a judge playing poker.

Jamie looks satisfied on the sidelines, and why wouldn't he? We're playing some genuinely good stuff, piling on the pressure and pressing high up the field. We nick the ball back in their half, Boothy nods a header agonizingly wide and the crowd applaud appreciatively.

'Told you we're much better,' says Dad bullishly.

Dad has tempted fate and angered the football gods and there can now only be one outcome. We're approaching the half-hour mark and, despite being utterly dominant, the Edward Hyde side to our Henry Jekyll makes himself known. There's a comical goal-line scramble out of nowhere and the referee awards a penalty to Whitby. I don't know if it's the right or wrong decision but we do our bit and scream blue murder at the referee, labelling it the worst decision ever and generally jumping up and down oozing faux fury.

'Are you blind, ref?' screams club president Reginald Timpkins, squinting through his thick-lensed specs.

Jamie is incandescent and hurls abuse at a pretty terrified fourth official who I'm sure couldn't see what happened either. The usually placid Sandy goes totally spare, shooting out of the technical area to let the 'man in black' know what he thinks. It's all for nothing though: the decision stands and our assistant manager/substitute is awarded an immediate yellow card.

I take this moment to test whether my pocket programme is a bringer of good or bad fortune. As their player places the ball on the spot I clutch it with all my might. 'Miss, miss, miss,' I chant yearningly to myself, gripping the battered little A5 booklet, hoping to harness its possible powers and do to penalties what Uri Geller did to spoons.

The crowd jeer as the Whitby player backs away from the ball and a brief moment of nervousness flashes across his sweaty face.

'Miss, miss, miss,' I repeat pleadingly, feeling the magic of the programme doing its work as my buttocks clench in anticipation.

Our keeper moves side to side and the ref blows his whistle. There's a moment of dramatic silence as the Whitby player takes a long run-up before scoring comfortably.

'Bollocks!' I shout uselessly into the wind before running inside and putting the now proven-to-be-cursed programme behind the bar and as far away from the action as possible.

There are fifteen minutes left of the first half and I find myself cast back into a role I've played before: the ineffective cheerleader. I do my bit as I clap, encourage and shriek to absolutely no avail as our lads compete in a game of who can miss the clearest chance quickest. It's a close one: they're all elite-level competitors when it comes to missing sitters. Boothy blasts well over the bar, the experienced Liam Tomsett heads centimetres wide, then the fit-again Connor Hughes squanders an open goal. It's possibly the worst miss in the history of the game. It's so bad it's almost impressive. He looks down at the turf and blames an invisible bobble, but there's no hiding place and he runs back to his position redfaced. I fall to my knees and whimper unstoically as the first half is brought to a close.

I can feel my panic levels rising and I'm desperate to avoid any half-time conversation, knowing that an interaction with

Larry or any opinionated supporter could push me over the edge. I feel like the only way the evening could get worse is if I break down in tears in front of the visiting directors. I decide to do what any sensible adult would do and take the spare key from the secretary's office and hide in the outside storage unit. Locked away in the icy cold shipping container I gather my thoughts and start to consider my next move. I start to feel much calmer, until Dale opens the unit to find me sat in the dark squashed against a disused hotplate, a ball bag and multiple packets of unopened socks. He takes a canister of Deep Heat and an old knee support and closes me back in. It's a moment we'll never mention to each other again.

The second half is much of the same, with even more firepower brought on from the bench. We throw everything at Whitby except the blocked kitchen sink. I start to get the feeling there's a better chance of me winning *Bake Off* than of us scoring. The gods are pissed off and Lady Luck seems to persistently frown on us as we have shot after shot blocked, stopped or defeated by the woodwork.

'Come on!' screams Dad in uncontrolled anguish as another shot is dragged hopelessly wide.

'Christ,' moans Deano through gritted teeth as Whitby clear the ball off the line.

The clock's running down and I'm starting to wish I had stayed in the storage unit. The ball cannons off the post to deny us again, and my stomach drops as I sense the patience around the ground wearing thin. Cheers give way to jeers as Boothy fails to connect with another cross, then to add salt to the increasingly gaping wound the ref denies us a stonewall penalty.

There are just ten minutes left to play and Whitby have brought on two defenders and parked a whole series of double deckers. We huff and puff but we just can't find a way through.

I'm in bits, my throat is hoarse, and I have so much adrenalin in my body I feel like I want to punch someone, or myself. We've done more than enough to win today and we look set to leave with nothing. I feel awful for our volunteers, who have worked tirelessly all day to get the pitch ready after multiple home games. A couple of supporters start to head to the exits and I contemplate the long drive back south.

Then suddenly, when all appears lost, Shezza plays an incisive through ball to Connor who beats the defender and advances down the wing. The match snaps into slow motion as he cuts inside from the right and squares the ball to the soon-to-be-incarcerated Niall Somerset. It's the stuff of Hollywood redemption movies. Niall takes a touch, shoots, and blasts the ball into the top corner.

I embrace Dad and we literally jump with joy, waving our arms aloft and screaming in delight. It's a huge goal. We've been the better side and we've been rewarded for our efforts.

'Get in!' I shout, punching the air triumphantly. It's only a draw but this one feels like a win. After so much disappointment I'm determined to savour the moment. The result will mean we're six unbeaten and on a bit of a roll.

I turn to Dad to continue our celebrations but his face has turned leaden and ghostlike. I follow his eyeline and immediately understand why. The flag is up and the goal has been disallowed.

'He was miles onside, you pillock!' Reginald protests.

I cover my eyes in disbelief as a sense of injustice burns at my cheeks. After such elation it's so cruel to be robbed by an incorrect decision.

'He was onside,' mumbles Dad softly to himself.

The match continues but the fight has gone out of the team. We've been collectively delivered a knockout blow, and the final minutes of the match ebb away into the night.

Full time. Ashton United 0 Whitby Town 1.

A corner has not been turned, our luck has not changed, and more of the same has been served up. It's the usual cocktail of (at times) fantastic football mixed with a splash of failure to convert chances and a dash of ineptitude in the back four. Our supporters are gutted and make their way home or to the bar to commiserate. Most of them stay to applaud the team's efforts, but two cagouled figures behind the goal boo loudly. I slump against the wooden balustrade and let out a cry of impotent rage.

'How have we lost that?' whines Dad, his eyes bleary and weary and possibly teary. 'We've got to start taking our chances.'

A huge part of me wants to shout 'No shit, Sherlock!' but we're making an effort to get on so I just about muster, 'That's a good point.'

We watch the team trudge back like zombies to the changing rooms as a familiar feeling of melancholy settles on the soul of Hurst Cross.

We shake hands solemnly with the visiting directors, emptily wishing them the best. Reginald slowly walks inside to get warm as the post-match waltz of ongoing maintenance begins once again.

Suddenly my blood runs cold as I feel hot breath inside my ear.

'Time for change,' Larry whispers as he walks past into the directors' box.

At least we know who @A56UTDB is.

'He's probably right, too,' I think to myself.

11

As Bad as It Gets?

I'm dressed as a five-year-old child, wearing bright green-and-yellow overalls and holding a novelty-sized teddy bear. I'm alone in my shared dressing room at the theatre with the door locked. I can hear my friends joking and laughing over the tannoy after a good matinée performance. I, on the other hand, feel like my heart has been scooped out and stomped on by an elephant. I'm collapsed on a sofa, head bowed, looking down at my phone and staring at the full-time score.

Ashton United 2 Spennymoor 6.

We've crashed out of the FA Cup in the third qualifying round and the faint hope that a run in the competition could rescue our faltering season is over. It's dawning on me that without a radical change our first season in charge is set to be a total failure, and it's only October!

All that remains on the horizon is the grim prospect of a likely relegation battle. I feel a cold shudder run through my body as, for the first time, I entertain a thought I have not allowed myself to think. What if we go down? What if our first season is the club's second successive relegation and we drop down to our lowest level in twenty-eight years? It's unthinkable but undeniably possible.

It's still early days, but we're now close to a third of the way through the season and we're currently fourth from bottom and only just outside the drop zone. Our supporters don't deserve this. It was only three months ago that I promised adventure and the best football they'd ever seen, and all we've delivered is pain. I feel like a fraud. I've spent the last hour locked in terror as my negative thoughts move around in circles. The more I try to break the cycle and think about something else, the more I helplessly ruminate on our current situation, my shortcomings and the future for the club.

The blood rushes to my head and I start to feel dizzy. Today's result is an impossibly hard one to stomach for a number of reasons, not least because after forty minutes we were 2–1 up and on top of the match. I'd checked my phone during the interval and seen that after initially going behind we'd scored a worldie of an equalizer before Boothy put away a tap-in for us to take the lead. Victory would have put us within ninety minutes of the first round proper and the chance of a mouth-watering tie with a professional league side. It would have given us something to build on, not to mention a guaranteed £8,750 even if we lost in the next round. I'd gone downstairs to finish the show full of beans, only for us then to concede on average every ten minutes, leaving me and our supporters devastated.

A wave of anxiety crashes over me as my heart starts pounding. I know what's coming but I don't have the fight or presence of mind to do anything about it. My phone pings constantly as new messages come thick and fast.

Jamie: *Sorry all, our performance was unacceptable. We will get it right.*

Dad: *You missed a shocker. Just awful. (Sad face emoji, angry face emoji, green sick face emoji)*

Robbo in our board WhatsApp group: *That was embarrassing. Turgid again.*

Another from Dad – *Call me when you can* – plus three missed calls.

My fiancée Lucy: *How was your day? Love you x*

Debby: *We don't have enough players for women's match tomorrow. Any ideas?*

Ryan (Juniors coach): *Can the under fifteens use the pitch tomorrow we have nowhere to play?*

Mum: *Your dad is very stressed please call him when you get a moment. PS we were crap today. (Crying face emoji)*

Deano: *Hello Jonathan, I have several practical issues that need your attention.*

Flash: *I have an amazing baller for you. He will solve all your problems! Snooze you lose.*

I scroll through the Twitter and Facebook comments in digital self-flagellation. It's brutal.

Time for change.

Dreadful season continues.

What a load of shit!

I know our fans are supportive and understanding but I can't help but be pulled into a habit of gauging the temperature of the town via three or four people who constantly take to their keyboards to vent their anger.

I feel my blood pressure surging as my breath gets shorter. My chest tightens as I battle with my ribcage to inhale, tugging at the buttons on my adult-size playsuit and discarding my teddy bear. I know that I'm starting to have a panic attack but there's nothing I can do. A very real pain shoots up my breastbone as a dull ache moans in my ears, flooding my brain with jets of white noise.

An increasingly familiar voice pops up in my head, chastising me: 'Look what you've done, you idiot. This is your fault.'

I'm letting everyone down. I need to do something.

I get up hurriedly and stagger to the sink, splashing my face liberally with water. I'm intent on action but totally unsure of what I can do, especially from so far away and with another show to do later this evening. I suck the air from the room hungrily, trying to find some kind of release. An invisible rope wraps around my chest as my stomach sinks like an anchor.

'This is your fault,' says the voice, this time more scornfully.

I need to do something. I've got to do something.

Breathless, I grab my phone and fire out messages to all the different stupid self-created group chats.

Hard luck, Jamie. We'll bounce back. Send.

Breathe, two, three, four . . .

Wipe my eyes.

'You're crying, you're pathetic,' scolds the voice.

I need to do something.

'Breathe, four, five, six,' I tell myself as I fire off another text.

Don't give up. We'll get there. (Smiley face emoji, weird flirty winky face emoji) Delete weird flirty winky face and send.

That's a shame. Sounded like we were great first half. Send.

Will call soon, been on stage. Send.

I feel like there's a sponge blocking my throat and airways.

I struggle against it, burbling a little as I desperately loosen my overalls in an attempt to untie the invisible rope. I take a sip of water but start coughing uncontrollably.

My day is going great baby. How about you? Love you too x. Send.

Not sure about players. Where are the current ones? Send.

I think you can. Check with Deano. Why don't you have anywhere to play? Send.

Will call him soon. (Smiley face emoji) Send.

Okay. Will call and sort later. Send.

The whirring in my head begins to subside as I lie back on the sofa and try to catch my sprinting breath.

Still, I've got to do something.

I turn on the mindfulness app on my phone and, still half dressed like I'm ready to go to nursery, begin to listen and try to meditate. A friendly and serene voice tells me to focus on exhaling. She tells me that I shouldn't fight negative thoughts but rather observe them like cars driving by on the road. She says that sometimes there will be very few cars on the road, whereas other times there might be a little traffic that will eventually pass. I think it's fair to say that right now, after a rough week at the club, the road is gridlocked.

It's been confirmed by the league that we'll be docked a point and we're waiting for the news to be made public. Plus we've been threatened with a fine by the league compliance officer for not correctly displaying the league sponsor BetVictor on our website. We've also been told we'll need to age-gate our website because of the enforced clickable links to the betting site. I think it's utterly mad that we, along with every other club at tier seven, are being forced to advertise mass gambling sites, but we have no choice, and arguing that doing this is against my principles doesn't help.

'You've got no convictions,' rebukes the voice once again.

There have been more frantic ins and outs of playing personnel. A new striker has arrived and another one has left. We're now on our third keeper of the season after our second more reliable keeper got injured. On the pitch a lucky draw against local rivals Hyde and a 4–0 victory over basement boys Grantham hasn't been enough to lift the gloom that has gathered over the last couple of months. It's not helped by the fact that our home form is far worse than our away form, meaning most of our supporters haven't seen a league win in over six months!

My phone pings again, interrupting my attempts to find nirvana, this time with a message from Angie: *Hope you're both OK. Could have done with the prize money today. We're low on cash for wages this week.* I let out another cry of despair and throw my phone across the dressing room.

There's a knock on my door.

'Just a minute,' I say as sunnily as I can, sniffing and wiping my eyes.

'Everything all right in there, Jon?' asks one of my colleagues.

'Absolutely,' I lie.

'OK. Just, there's a lot of screaming going on in your room.'

'Sorry, I just saw the football result. Bit frustrating, haha.'

'Right . . . Going out for a bit.'

I open my laptop and log in to internet banking, still panting as I click through into my savings account.

I close my Mac and pick my phone back up, typing another WhatsApp message as I flop back on to the sofa.

I've transferred enough to cover this week's payroll. Send.

I consider restarting the mindfulness recording when my phone rings. It's Dad. It must be the fifth time he's called in twenty minutes. I know he means well but I'm starting to feel suffocated by his constant phone calls. I'm desperately aware that I have another show in an hour and the last thing I need is a blow-by-blow account of how bad we were, but I do my best to compose myself and pick up.

'Hello,' I say.

'Hello,' he replies glumly. 'Did you see the score?'

'I did. I've followed it all on Twitter.'

'We lost 6–2,' he says, as if I hadn't spoken. 'We were 2–1 up and we just capitulated.'

'I know,' I tell him.

'We're out of the FA Cup now,' he adds morosely.

'I know, Dad.'

'We could have done with winning that. We'd have got almost nine grand.'

'Jesus, I know all this. I can see it!'

'All right, I'm just trying to keep you in the loop,' he says, sounding hurt.

'You're not keeping me in the loop, you're just repeating shit news on a loop. There's a difference. I know we lost. I know we got hammered. And I know we were winning and that we won't get the prize money!'

'And we're out of the FA Cup,' he repeats.

Dad starts to talk about how we need to be more compact

and pragmatic at the back but I can't bear to listen. He starts to describe each goal we conceded in detail but I just can't take it.

'I don't have time to talk about this,' I say bluntly.

'Oh, right,' he says.

'I've got to go.'

I hang up, and immediately feel incredibly guilty and regret being so harsh. I know the situation is even harder for Dad. He lives round the corner from the ground and never gets a minute's peace. He gives so much of his time to the club and he's not missed a game yet, so days like today must sting even more for him. We were supposed to be doing this together. It was supposed to be fun. The least I could have done is been a supportive ear to bend. Instead I've behaved like a spoilt brat.

'You handled that well,' chides the voice in my head.

I fall back on to the sofa and curl up in the foetal position, utterly distraught. Tears roll down my face as I sob despairingly.

'Are you sure you're OK?' says my colleague from outside the door, having returned with her dinner. 'It sounds like you're weeping quite a lot?'

'Yeah, still checking the football results.'

'OK. Must be a bad one,' she adds, walking off.

I listen to her footsteps fade away then slide down to the floor, wiping my eyes with my novelty sleeve. I know that something needs to change and it needs to change quickly. Despite a couple of wins we're still incredibly inconsistent and I can't see a situation where that changes with things as they are.

We've changed the team, the formation and our keeper three times, and as much as I don't want to, my head is starting to tell me that we now need to change the manager. Maybe we should have done it at the board meeting weeks ago. We need to find a way to wrest back the feel-good factor at the club and at the very least ensure our position in the league.

I start to type a new message.

For a brief moment, I am decided. That is until my heart gets in the way and I revert to being undecided. Is this really Jamie's fault? We've had bad luck with injuries and with individual errors. Will a change in manager fix that? I certainly don't want us to sack someone just so we can feel like we're being proactive. Maybe we just need to wait and allow more time for Jamie's philosophy to bed in? After all, if the goal against Whitby had been given this would have been our first defeat in eight, and that's not bad at all.

I delete the message and sit deep in thought. Hoping for a sign but knowing one won't come. We need to work this out ourselves and we're not going to get any help.

If we change the manager then maybe things will turn around and at the very least we can wipe the slate clean and start again. That said, so many of our players are contracted that anyone coming in is going to have one hand tied behind their back. It's also going to take at least a fortnight to find someone and we have games coming up thick and fast. Is now the right time to play at least four matches with a caretaker manager in place, or worse, no manager in place?

Perhaps we've hit rock bottom and the only way from here is up? Perhaps the best course of action is to wait and see? I just don't really know. The only thing I'm certain of is that falling out with Dad isn't going to help.

I type out another message: *Sorry for being an arse. We'll get there. (Smiley face emoji)* Send.

I breathe deeply and sigh heavily.

Message from Dad: *I know. Bloody hard though isn't it.*

I think if we don't win in the next three games then it is time for change. Send.

Message from Dad: *(Cucumber emoji)*

Message from Dad: *Sorry accident. Meant this.*

Message from Dad: *(Thumbs-up emoji)*

I feel a little better. We've not made a decision but we've at least decided on when we might make a decision in the future.

I send another message, this time to Deano. *Please send practical requests to Dad, or anyone else. I have no idea how to deal with any of them.* Send.

Then a final one to Flash. *Can the baller fix TVs or do DIY?* Send.

Immediate response from Flash: *Yes, he's a joiner. He says he'll do it for an extra £50 per week.*

I turn my phone off and try to focus. We need a win, Jamie needs a win. It's time to get a handle on the mess. It's time to be proactive and to be an adult.

I zip up my playsuit, pick up my teddy bear and head down to the stage.

12

Rollercoaster Recap

It's now 23 November and I'm back at Hurst Cross for the first time in three weeks to see us play Nantwich Town. It's an absolute must-win game.

I've arrived early feeling tired and grumpy. Last night I was woken up at 2 a.m. by my phone going into overdrive. Distressingly, a new WhatsApp group is off and running. This one is simply called 'Operation Glitter Roll'. To my profound sadness, I quickly learnt the purpose of this group is to discuss the ground grading work that must be completed on the outdoor gents' toilets. The main issues, according to the paper circulated by the league compliance officer, are a broken flush, poor general hygiene and a lack of running water. It's also been discovered that there are hundreds of empty Carling cans hidden above the ceiling panels, which could give way at any moment. Carling don't do ceiling insulation, and if they did it would seem they would cause a massive health and safety issue. How the cans got there nobody knows but they need to be removed immediately. If all the work isn't sorted by March we will be penalized and could even be automatically relegated. I'm determined to make sure that if we do go down it will be due to the quality of the football and not the state of our urinals.

There's been a growing sense of distrust in the camp of late. A couple of weeks ago we were fined £100 for wearing the incorrect training bibs during warm-up on a match day. It's the third time something like this has happened and it sent shock waves through the club. As an ex-police officer, Robbo has been particularly exercised by the whole affair as he tends to be triggered by minor infractions of league guidelines. The league compliance officer has sent photographic evidence of each of our transgressions so it would appear that someone is coming to all our games and filming or photographing our warm-ups and what our management staff and substitutes are wearing on the bench. The photos are all from home games and some appear to have been taken from the changing rooms. It's led to rumours that there's a mole within the club. Robbo has taken it upon himself to turn detective, interviewing everyone at length. He's watched back hundreds of hours of CCTV footage from the secret cameras set up by Deano earlier in the season and has vowed to find the culprit.

I look around the ground and, considering we're only ten minutes from kick-off, the place feels quieter than normal and it's not just me who's in a bad mood. The fans that *have* come seem subdued and listless but there are also a lot of people missing. It could be that they just don't fancy braving the weather but I fear it could be down to some of the events of the last few weeks. A lot has happened and a lot has changed. It's been a month of twists and turns that I've had to observe from a distance after being away on honeymoon.

The outdoor bar is once again open for business (just in time for winter), this time with the council's blessing. Dad has also begun work on renovating our indoor bar, which he has promised to turn into a modern sports bar before Christmas. I've asked to be part of the design process for this and he says I will be, but I can tell I won't.

Unfortunately we've been the victim of a series of break-ins, and although nothing has been taken, a mysterious hooded figure has written 'AUFC ARE SHIT' on the back of the Popular Stand. A small army led by Deano have tried to wash the wall clean but to little avail. The only letters that have budged after hours of soap and hot water application are the A, the F and the C, meaning the wall now reads 'U ARE SHIT'.

Our women's team has also started to hit a run of bad form, although this has largely been down to a battle to keep team numbers high enough. A frustrating blend of injuries, university timetables, changed work rotas and a particularly nasty bereavement has meant that in our last three matches we've only been able to field ten players. This has included a 7–1 humiliation at the hands of our rivals Mossley. We're back to begging for new players on Twitter and hoping we can make it through the winter period without having to forfeit games.

Meanwhile, the rapid-fire revolving door of playing personnel has continued to turn for our men's team at breakneck speed, including the arrival of a new central midfielder, Andrew Howarth, who goes straight into the starting eleven despite not having met the squad until an hour ago. Tarantula has also reclaimed his position as our number one. And Jamie remains at the wheel. Our results have continued to be inconsistent but just about consistent enough to feel that it would be unfair to remove him from his long-held position in the hot seat.

After the FA Cup demolition, we played away to lower-league local rivals Droylsden in the Manchester Premier Cup. Jamie decided to prioritize the league, naming a much-changed side including a first start for our assistant manager Sandy, who made his mark by scoring the only goal of the game after sixty-two minutes. Unfortunately for us it was in his own net and we bowed out of the county cup at the first hurdle. I couldn't make it that night but it sounds like I didn't miss much in a match that, according to several reports, lacked intensity and chances and was described mostly as 'far too cold to be outside'. The general apathy towards the tie from everyone, seemingly including the opposition, meant that we discounted the fixture from being part of the three games that would decide Jamie's future at the club.

Our next match was away at high-flying Lancaster where we may have hit rock bottom. The earlier choice to rest players did nothing and we were utterly awful in every single way. We registered no shots on target and were very lucky to lose 3–0.

Although the result was one to forget, it was a match that will be best remembered for the animosity shown towards Jamie as our supporters made their feelings known. Just before the match, Aaron Chalmers was officially released and a group of fans spent the entirety of the ninety minutes berating our already under-fire manager. They started drunk and angry and by the time we were 1–0 down they were hammered and livid. The final whistle was greeted by chants of 'You're getting sacked in the morning' and 'You don't know what you're doing'. Dad was crestfallen and left early with Mum. Our

Facebook and Twitter pages were packed with demands that Jamie be sacked immediately, with several supporters vowing not to return until the change had been made.

I then received a call early in the morning from our goal-keeper coach Killian who was both shaken and stirred after the match. He said that some of our fans' behaviour had got out of hand post-match, with Sandy being confronted by a small but lairy section of ultras in the car park. Additionally, while the players were showering, an inebriated Stella managed to break into the changing room to tell the lads they were a disgrace and to bang her drum at them.

A few days later we were back in action and backed up the previous result with a heartbreaking defeat away at Witton Albion. After Stella's entry into the changing room it was Dad's turn this time. He popped in before the match to deliver an impassioned speech backing the team and giving them his support to turn things round. There was a real togetherness and fighting spirit for the full ninety minutes, tragically under-cut by a Cesaire Lingouba stunner in the ninety-first minute, condemning us to a fourth successive defeat. The result saw us fall into the relegation zone for the first time with our point deduction still to come into effect.

Things were so bleak that I reached out to Flash to see if he could help. He immediately sent lots of WhatsApp videos with different players scoring lots of goals from many angles. I said that I'd pass them on to our manager as we were des-perate for a goalscorer. He replied saying that he didn't have a goalscorer on his books at the moment and the client he was suggesting was the goalkeeper in the videos. Apparently it's the same guy, and if you look past all the goals he's conceding he's actually very agile. I vowed never to contact Flash again.

Then, when things were at their darkest and the axe was finally about to fall, Jamie changed our formation. The dawn came, and with it a stay of execution. We ripped Gainsborough Trinity apart, winning 3–1, and backed it up with a 1–0 win in the FA Trophy first qualifying round, with Shezza scoring a screamer. Hot on the heels of this came a 2–1 win over fellow strugglers Buxton, courtesy of two penalties from Josh Wilson. After that match I headed off on honeymoon feeling, for the first time in a long while, that we were heading in the right direction. I watched Jamie's post-match interview online and he looked the closest to relaxed I had seen him since the start of the season. The league table also looked a whole lot healthier, with us five points away from trouble. As Lucy and I got on to the plane I even allowed myself to fantasize about an unlikely dash for the play-offs.

I followed results carefully while away, which sadly saw the new dawn prove to be a false one. Heavy rain meant our next league game was postponed, before we then lost 1–0 away to Matlock in the second qualifying round of the FA Trophy. Shortly after this game our point deduction was also made public and applied to the table, meaning we were once again only two points from the drop zone.

With a run of home games coming up and the pitch in a fragile condition, we brought in an outside contractor to help keep games on. He made the alarming decision to drive a tractor down one side of our completely sodden pitch. Rather than fixing whatever he was trying to fix, the tractor ripped into the left-hand side of the turf, leaving huge tyre marks in its wake. This means we'll probably need to re-lay the entire pitch at the end of the season at a cost of thousands of pounds. It also means that passing the ball and keeping it on the deck is going to be impossible on the left-hand side of the pitch.

To add insult to injury we lost to our bitter foes Stalybridge Celtic for a second time in the season, this time succumbing to defeat in the Integro League Cup first round at home. A need to protect players for the next league game and a sudden injury crisis saw Jamie attempt to get the game called off before being forced to name himself as a substitute. At 2–0 down with twenty minutes to play and a goal looking incredibly unlikely, Jamie made the bold decision to sub himself on, replacing his assistant Sandy who had again been asked to start. Another late Josh Wilson penalty on ninety minutes was our only con-solation in a game that was branded online as 'embarrassing'. The defeat meant we were out of all the many cups we were eligible to play in, including the FA Cup, the FA Trophy and the Manchester Cup.

Today we find ourselves without a win in two but still hav-ing won our last two league games. Victory today would mean three league wins on the bounce for the first time this season, but if we lose we're without a victory in three and back into crisis management (and most likely the bottom three).

We're about to kick off, but something doesn't feel right. I can't put my finger on it but the atmosphere feels simultane-ously flat and hostile. There's a kind of apathy as the players run out to a muted smattering of applause. I look towards Jamie, who also seems subdued. He's sat on the bench with his hands in his pockets looking down at his shoes like a naughty schoolchild. Sandy looks similarly downtrodden. You'd have thought we were losing with only minutes left on the clock rather than just about to start. Boothy and Josh Wilson have also been mysteriously dropped and sit sulkily in our rusty dugout.

I feel an odd sensation rush over me, a combination of fear and guilt. I do my best to shake it off, and thankfully the whistle blows and we're underway. There's a little cheering from the crowd but it's much tamer than usual.

From the very start we look awkward and under-confident. We just can't keep the ball, and when we have it we pass it sideways without any cutting edge. Nantwich, on the other hand, look really dangerous. As the match wears on they stretch our defence, finding space all over the park. Their forward hits a warning shot that fizzes just over the bar and I can tell it's only a matter of time before they score. Shezza is out of sorts and Connor seems off the boil. There's an element of going through the motions and an odd sense of inevitability in the air, almost as if the team are expecting to lose.

We're caught in possession and Jamie rushes to the edge of his technical area to lay into someone, but our player uses some pretty industrial language to let him know that his feedback is not required. There's a couple of ironic cheers from the crowd but mostly it's uncomfortable. Jamie sits back in the dugout with a face like thunder. Then, within five minutes, it's groundhog day. One of our defenders clatters into their striker in the box and the referee gives a penalty which is dispatched by their midfielder James Lawrie with ease. There's an enervated silence in the ground, broken only by the enthusiastic cheering of the twenty or so Nantwich fans who have made the journey, no doubt sensing an enjoyable afternoon ahead.

We have a few chances but nothing clear-cut and Tarantula does well to keep the score at 1–0. Then, as is becoming routine, disaster strikes. New boy Andrew Howarth jumps two-footed into a challenge that would be more at home in a UFC cage fight and is shown an immediate red card. He looks to the skies in exasperation but it's a horrible tackle that he didn't need to make. He storms straight down the tunnel and into the changing room never to be seen again, quite literally. It's the first and last time he will play for us in a club career spanning forty-three minutes. Jamie and Sandy watch on without much emotion, and soon the half-time whistle blows, giving us momentary release. There are a couple of boos but for the most part the crowd disperse noiselessly to the bar, keen to get out of the rain and away from the football.

I head into the directors' lounge where Dad, Angie and Robbo stand in a huddle not saying much while Larry and Reginald sit sombrely in the corner sipping from large tumblers of whisky. Larry gives me a glare of dissatisfaction but he doesn't elaborate and doesn't need to. The Nantwich directors suppress their glee, picking up on the sense of sadness that seems to have enveloped the ground.

A woman in a Nantwich blazer comes up to me and puts a supportive arm on my shoulder.

'Bloody football, eh?' she says.

I smile and nod. I get the sense she's gone through all this before.

'It's the hope that kills you, love,' she says compassionately before heading to the soup urn.

I drift into the bar and look around. Everybody is sat at their usual tables mournfully, resigned to another home loss.

I don't think it's the hope that's killing us, it's the lack of it. We've only won one league game here all season so I can't blame them. I feel an immense pang of shame as I head out back towards the pitch for the second half. I catch Dad's eye. He looks suitably bereft as he zips his coat up securely, ready to endure the next forty-five minutes.

Jamie must be feeling the importance of the game because he's made three substitutions. Despite going down to ten men, he's brought on three attacking players with Liam Tomsett, Josh Wilson and Boothy all on the field of play.

I prepare myself for a nerve-racking half of missed chances but it's nothing like that. Our bubble is burst straight away as their number ten Callum Saunders slots home after fifty minutes, giving us an Everest-sized mountain to climb. We're a man and two goals down and it's clear that we're going to lose, it's just a question of how many they'll score. A couple of our supporters head back into the bar as the heavens start to weep on Hurst Cross.

There are mini arguments breaking out among the team as they start to blame one another, and the anger is turned up a notch when Saunders bags his second of the game. If this was boxing we'd throw in the towel, but sadly it's not so we have to continue with twenty minutes left on the clock as punches crash down on us from all sides. Sandy claps and does what he can to motivate the lads but it's a lost cause. Just three minutes later ex-Premier League star Ricardo Fuller turns back the clock and bags a goal from an impossibly tight angle after a mazy run through our box, making the score 4–0.

I squat down on the decking as the rain now lashes down with biblical fury, bouncing angrily on to the terraces and the darkening concrete in thick droplets. Thunder rumbles with irritation as the pitch becomes sludgier by the second. The young linesman nearest to us looks at his watch longingly, desperate to get inside with a brew.

I'm drenched but hardly aware of it. I just feel numb. There's a sourness curdling in the air and suddenly the ground feels devoid of goodwill. Stella beats her drum as five or six supporters behind the goal join in a rendition of 'sacked in the morning'. Tom, Bethany and the rest of the crowd by the dugout vocalize their displeasure too. Every lost ball is followed by shouts of 'Switch on!' and every time the opposition pass through they're on the players' backs. Even the eternally jovial Dale looks like he's chewing a bag of wasps and screams 'Get a grip for God's sake!' as another spat breaks out between players on our own team.

Things are starting to turn toxic as complaints give way to rage. More and more people are leaving early as our Ashton United dissolves into Ashton Divided. Our supporters have got behind the team in every match I've been at, regardless of how we've played, so it's gut-wrenching now to see everyone so unhappy. It's way more uncomfortable than if there was a stadium full of thousands revolting en masse. This is more intimate and much more personal. I can recognize each dissenting voice and know each crestfallen face. It's not a sea of people, it's a tiny pond, and we all know and like one another.

Nantwich hit the post and a few more supporters join the growing exodus. They head to the exit, mumbling and grumbling. Some shout 'time for change' as they walk past us. There's less than three minutes to go now and less than a hundred people in the ground. I don't know if it's pity or fatigue but even the Nantwich players have stopped trying. Everyone is just waiting for the match to be over so we can thaw out and get home. Jamie and Sandy sit at the back of the dugout, their AUFC dark-red coats zipped over their mouths, their foreheads wrinkled in discomfort. Surely they know the writing is on the wall? And I'm not talking about the graffiti.

After what feels like an eternity the final whistle blows, but this time nobody is put out of their misery. There are no boos or jeers, just an eerie cloak of quiet that covers the ground. The players trudge off, shame-faced and mud-soaked. Jamie looks towards the main stand before walking slowly down the tunnel. The kitmen carry out their rituals, emptying out the half-drunk water bottles and picking up the damp and discarded tracksuits from the dugout.

Dad and I watch on dumbstruck as Robbo, Angie and Deano head back inside. A few supporters come over to confront us.

'We've got to get rid!' shouts one young fan in my direction.

'You two are sound, but he's dragging you down,' says his interchangeable friend.

'You've got to give him the bloody sack,' snaps Frank Taunton, who's back watching today after another self-imposed exile.

Dad doesn't reply, whereas all I can do is nod softly in submission, closing my eyes in the hope that it's all a bad dream.

'If you don't do it, I will,' snaps another man in a tracksuit.

I don't know how that would work but I briefly wish he would. The truth is I'm still terrified of Jamie, and the idea of having to remove him from his post fills me with dread. I shudder a little as Larry appears out of nowhere accompanied by what must be the wettest dog ever.

'I've seen some crap in the last forty years, but that takes the cake and the biscuit,' he says bitingly. He staggers towards the door before turning for dramatic effect, looking us both dead in the eye through the incessant rain. 'I know you don't want to do it, but you have to,' he says urgently. 'Nice doesn't get you anywhere in football,' he adds before disappearing inside, closing the door with a thump.

We stand in the rain, contemplating the inevitable. We've got to make the change and we've got to do it soon. After today's performance it's hard to see where our next goal might come from, let alone a win.

Dad places his hand on my shoulder and smiles gently.

'Let's get out of the rain,' he says.

I look across the ground with a heavy heart and a soggy soul. I've had some low moments in the last few months but this is hands down the worst. The pitch looks like a war zone and the only positive I can think of is that if the rain carries on, our next match might be postponed and we can have two weeks' respite. The corners of the ground have started to flood and more letters of the graffiti on the back of the Popular Stand have washed away in the downpour: the U, the A, the R and the E.

The wall now simply reads SHIT.

'Indeed,' I think to myself.

13

The Break-up

I have been rehearsing all morning, re-running exactly what I'm going to say and practising each sombre intonation.

'This is a results industry,' I say to myself in the mirror, 'and sadly, results aren't where they need to be.'

As you can probably guess, I'm not preparing for a performance but rather for a difficult conversation. It's been two days since our mauling at the rough hands of mid-table Nantwich and both Dad and I, as well as the entire town of Ashton, have come to the conclusion that Jamie must go. In fairness we've probably arrived at the decision a little later than others.

There's been a growing undercurrent of disharmony at the club for a number of weeks if not months now, and I'm frustrated it's taken us so long to act. We've had a few good results on the way, but in reality they've barely papered over the cracks of a bad season and a breakdown between those on the terraces and on the pitch. We need to recapture the mood of excitement that accompanied our joining the club before the end of the year.

Our social media has been bursting with comments demanding change but on top of the usual suspects there are more people discreetly, or in some cases anonymously, coming forward with their opinions. I've had personal messages from fans essentially entreating us to do something. This is in addition to a growing number of texts from players letting us know that their relationship with the gaffer has broken down. There have also been reports of a mass punch-up in the changing room after the match on Saturday, with several people now unable to be in the same room as one another, let alone on the same pitch.

The final nail in the gaffer's coffin came last night when I was contacted secretly by 'a whistle-blower' with a stark warning regarding how things are behind the scenes. He said it was his duty to come forward because things 'can't carry on as they are'. He told me that Jamie has been juggling a newborn baby and a fledgling business with his commitments to the club, and AUFC are often in last place. That he's trying his best but he just doesn't have the time to give what is needed to turn the ship around, especially with us drifting off course so rapidly. It's apparently causing disharmony among the squad who are being lambasted each week for not giving enough by a coach who they feel is too absent far too often.

All this coupled with our terrible form means there can only be one choice if we're going to salvage the campaign in any way. Unfortunately, Jamie, Dad and I are all in different places emotionally, but more importantly physically, so we're having to deliver the news via conference call. It's not ideal but it's clear that we have to act now.

It's a weird situation. We've wanted to do the honourable

thing and make sure Jamie is the first to know, but we've also had to prepare everything for after we've spoken to make sure we can move forward quickly. It doesn't feel especially pleasant but there's a lot to think about and we need to put the club first. We've got a match in five days' time and we're going to need an interim coach before we find our new manager. We're now just two points off the drop zone and urgently need someone who can change our fortunes quickly before any more damage is done. We also need to make sure the change is properly announced and that the league and FA are aware of our decision. Robbo is poised to tell our media team to put out a pre-written statement within the next twenty-five minutes and Angie is set to begin advertising the new position. I'm aware that we're a small town and news travels quickly so I don't want Jamie to learn about his fate through the grapevine.

'It's not you, it's me,' I say in the mirror before immediately deciding I will under no circumstances say this.

Despite being confident that we're making the correct decision I'm still absurdly nervous. I'm naturally very conflict-averse, and since I've known Jamie he's always been very conflict-positive, so I'm keen to do whatever I can to make sure it doesn't all kick off. I want to be clear but also compassionate and make sure Jamie can walk away with his head held high. Irrespective of how dire this season has been he's done a huge amount for the club so I'm keen to make this as painless as possible.

'You're fantastic, Jamie. It's just not working,' I say sincerely to the mirror.

'Who are you talking to, baby?' shouts my wife from across the hallway.

'Nobody,' I reply curtly.

'OK. It sounds like you're breaking up with someone in there.'

I look at the clock on the wall with a grimace. It's a few minutes to midday and the time has come. I take a deep breath, steady my trembling hands and dial in.

Dad is already waiting on the call. I can tell he's not looking forward to this either. He's monotone and monosyllabic which is always a giveaway that he's either furious or uncomfortable. There's also a massive delay on his end of the line, meaning everything feels slow and drawn-out, or that he accidentally cuts you off mid-sentence.

'Are you going to do the talking?' he asks apprehensively.

I agree that I will and we go through the various forms the call might take. I've done my prep and massively overthought everything. We both agree to do our best to avoid carrying out a complete autopsy of the season or getting stuck in an argument that won't do anyone any good. Then, after a few minutes of small talk, Jamie dials in.

'Afternoon both,' he says glumly.

'Afternoon,' I say.

There's a long pause.

'Morning,' says Dad.

I can feel myself breaking out into a sweat. I look in the mirror and see a red-faced fool fumbling for words.

'Thanks for joining us, Jamie,' I begin awkwardly, settling myself uneasily into my chair. 'I just wanted to start by letting you know how much we have appreciated your—'

'Thanks for joining,' Dad interrupts.

'Right,' says Jamie impatiently.

'I think we all agree that Saturday's match was really quite bad and that after some reflection as chairmen and as a board we—'

'It was very poor on Saturday,' adds Dad.

'Right,' says Jamie again.

I can feel my heart rate rising again and try my best to rip the plaster off rather than slowly tugging at it, making the experience more painful for all of us.

'Jamie, it's not you, it's me,' I blurt out, immediately disappointed in myself. 'Not me – us, the whole club. We need the results to improve, and while I know you're working hard I—'

This time it's Jamie's turn to interrupt, and he thankfully puts me out of my misery. 'It's OK, Jonathan, I know what you're trying to say. I've really enjoyed working with you and I'm gutted it's not worked out. There's no hard feelings.'

'It's a results business, Jamie, and we've decided to let you go,' adds Dad, still on a deeply inconvenient delay.

'I know, Dave,' says Jamie.

'Thanks, Jamie,' I say. 'We're gutted too.'

'I think I'm on a bit of a delay, lads,' says Dad.

'You are,' says Jamie.

'Yes, I'm also gutted,' adds Dad.

'Thanks, Dad,' I say.

'I am what?' says Dad.

'Delayed,' says Jamie.

I'm incredibly grateful for how gracious Jamie has been. He's not only taken the news well, in many ways I feel like he's helping us through the conversation. In fact he's so lovely about it that I start to question if we're doing the right thing. He says he's sad but it's par for the course in football management and that not everything can last for ever. He says he's grateful for the backing he's received and also admits that a break from the game and a chance to reset might not be the worst thing in the world.

'I won't have to be in all those WhatsApp groups any more,' he adds lightly.

We all laugh awkwardly for a moment before Jamie moves the conversation on.

'Have you already got someone lined up?' he asks.

'No,' I reply, 'we wouldn't do that. You're the only one who knows.'

'I hate those WhatsApp groups,' says Dad.

Jamie and I remain silent and wait for the lag on the line to catch up.

'Anyone there?' asks Dad after a couple of moments.

The man in the mirror slaps his forehead in frustration. I'm not sure if it's the delay or just the news sinking in a bit but I can sense Jamie is growing a little irritable. He lets us know that although he understands our decision he doesn't agree with it. He feels ultimately that he's been let down by players who haven't done the business for him and he just needed more time to 'bring in new blood' and 'move a few on'. He also argues that it was the club that encouraged him to contract so many of the squad, so changing personnel has been more difficult than it needed to have been. Finally, he points out that although we were 'dog shit' on Saturday our league form had been steadily improving.

I feel my face flush with more than a little vexation. Jamie was definitely keen to contract players and committed to a squad incredibly quickly. I can't help but think that he's not really taking responsibility for his choices and is just blaming everyone else around him. That said, I can see how I'm at least partly at fault and I'm keen to avoid getting into an argument.

'We just need to see the form turn around, Jamie,' I gently reason. 'I'm sorry, but look at our league position. The table doesn't lie.'

I immediately realize I shouldn't have said this and that I've opened the door for a blow-by-blow of the season. Jamie points out how unlucky we've been and how we could easily have had more points on the board. He says that it's not his fault strikers have missed chances and refs have been shit and argues that we've still got a lot of games in hand because we did 'well in the cups'. He's adamant that with a few new faces and a couple of lads back from injury we'd be back on track in a couple of weeks and challenging for promotion by the end of the season.

'It's not just the weekend that's been bad, we've been pretty crap for weeks,' Dad pipes up, taking the bait. 'I've said it time and time before but we've brought a lot of it on ourselves by tapping the ball about in our own backyard.'

I can feel my insides tightening. It's been going really well and I don't want us to end up fighting or talking in circles.

'It's not really important now,' I start to say.

'It is important,' Jamie counters. 'I want to play football, not just lump it.'

'We just need to get results,' I say as firmly as I can. 'Look, the situation is what it is and—'

'I'm not saying lump it,' Dad argues tardily.

I do my best to wrest back control of the conversation and

push us forward, past the relentless retrospectives and the delay on the line. Taking on the mantle of Mr Mediator I somehow manage to agree with both Jamie and Dad while also disagreeing at the same time. I let Jamie know that we're planning to put out a statement in the next half an hour and that we'll appoint a caretaker manager for the weekend. I thank him again for all his efforts, not just this season but before our time too.

Dad adds that he's always a phone call away if Jamie ever needs any help with his business or just friendly advice.

'You've done a huge amount for the club and I really do wish you all the best,' I say sincerely.

'You too,' says Jamie ruefully. 'Good luck with the rest of the season.'

And just like that it's done. I feel genuinely sad that it's not worked out but pleased to have done something proactive.

Dad messages Robbo and our media team to let them know they can put out our statement and begin the recruitment process.

I then call Sandy and let him know the news too. He'd already guessed and, as always, is admirably positive about the whole thing. He's not really up for staying while we find someone else and says 'him and the gaffer come as one'. He's wanted to cycle the Canadian Rockies for a number of years and this is the perfect opportunity.

'Best unpack the lycras,' he says, signing off.

I call the rest of the backroom team who are all similarly understanding and keen to do what's best for the club, and they each pledge to be at training and in the dugout on Saturday if required.

I then have a sudden crisis of confidence, worrying that we need to be more transparent with how we're running the club, and start calling round all our volunteers and ex-board members. I phone Larry, Tony, Reginald and Frank, who all seem rather nonplussed, before getting in touch with Dale, who also seems indifferent. After spending the next half an hour contacting everyone *else* I can think of, I realize all of them already knew the news somehow anyway.

I sit back on my office chair exhausted. I do genuinely feel more like I've just broken up with someone, and even though it was pretty amicable I feel a sense of emptiness. It's been an up-and-down few months and after the sense of excitement at the start of our relationship it stings that it's ended with us having to part ways. It also dawns on me that it's probably not the last time I'll have to have a conversation like this with a manager. I exhale deeply, but there's no time to relax and I start to contemplate what needs to happen next. We need someone who can arrest our sliding form and also bring everyone at the club together again.

Suddenly my phone springs to life. There's text after text from numbers I've never heard of. They're all from potential managers asking for a meeting or an interview. There are also a few messages from some of the playing squad, some letting me know that they agree with the decision and some asking to throw their hat in the ring for the top spot.

I log into my laptop and check my club emails. There are already forty-two CVs submitted and the advertisement has only been out for an hour.

'Shit,' I think to myself as a hundred questions start to flood my brain, all of which I can't answer. How are we going to choose a manager? How am I going to know which of these CVs is good? How will I know how to judge the answers we get in an interview? What kind of questions should I even be asking?

I get back on my laptop and start googling.

14

The Hunt is On

Another eight days have gone by and the post-Jamie era has begun.

A burst pipe has closed the outdoor bar until further notice and will no doubt entail further expense. The renovation of the indoor bar hit a snag when decades of large-scale electrical faults were unearthed, meaning the job is now less a touch-up and more a full rebuild. The finish date keeps getting pushed back but we're still hoping to reopen in two weeks for our home match against FC United of Manchester, a breakaway side formed by disenfranchised Manchester United fans during the Glazer takeover, for which we'll have a bumper crowd.

In other news I've been told we are running low on balls and the situation needs to be rectified ASAP. Apparently several have been kicked out of the ground during matches and training and have landed in various gardens. Normally we just identify the house, knock and, like little kids, ask for our ball back. Unfortunately a massively disproportionate number have landed in the backyard of one house on Rowley Street owned by a very angry woman who supports one of our local rivals and she's refused to give any of them back to us. It's got heated very quickly and we're now at loggerheads. Robbo has suggested we involve the police, saying that what's happening accounts to grand theft. Deano thinks we should break into her garden and steal the balls back. My suggestion to try to avoid reporting or committing crime by popping over with a bunch of flowers to de-escalate the issue was dismissed as naive and weak.

Sadly, the only improvement on the pitch since Jamie departed has been losing 3–0 at home rather than 4–0. This has left us hovering dangerously above the bottom three with only goal difference separating us from the dreaded drop zone. With the recruitment process for our new manager only just beginning, Josh Wilson took the reins as caretaker with the support of goalkeeper coach Killian in the dugout. The rest of Jamie's team ultimately decided to step away from the club and look for pastures new. A growing part of me wishes I could too.

The only sense of a silver lining is that the mole has now been found and we know who's been sending the incriminating photos to the league. The good news is we don't need to worry about it any more. The bad news is that it was accidentally me. Throughout the season I've been absent-mindedly taking photos around the ground and posting them on Twitter. I'd quite literally been publishing evidence of each of our offences on a weekly basis.

The week had started well with the team reportedly training much better and the mood in the camp improved. Dad even went down on the Thursday for moral support and to give a message of unity to the squad that he said was well received. I think he was quite proud of himself as he rang me on three separate occasions to give me a detailed account of exactly what he said, his speech to the lads becoming more Churchillian with each retelling.

Our supporters have also been revitalized, many of them taking to social media to guess who our next manager will be or to argue for their preferred candidate. Despite our beleaguered position I think it's fair to say everyone at the club had hoped that with the reset button firmly pressed we'd romp to a win at the weekend. Josh messaged me the night before we played to say the three points were as good as 'in the bag'. Our supporters clearly believed this too as a much larger crowd than the week before rushed through the turnstiles to watch. Sadly, the optimism proved to be misplaced and we were comprehensively beaten.

We started off well enough and played with new-found zip and enthusiasm but ultimately our opponents, Radcliffe, were both too strong and too well organized for us. They arrived with their tails in the air having won their last five matches and played with a confidence and fluidity we could only dream of. We were toe-to-toe for the first half hour, but after that it was the same old, same old for us with a triple helping of déjà vu being served up for our supporters with a side order of groundhog day. We wasted the chances we were able to create before an act of pure generosity from Tarantula saw Radcliffe take the lead two minutes before half-time. Any hopes of a spirited second-half turnaround were dashed when sloppy defending allowed their winger Tyrese Sinclair to score twice in quick succession on forty-six and fifty-four minutes, effectively ending the game. It's clear that even with an imminent change of manager there are still rifts and divisions within the team that need to be worked out. We're without a clear style of play or identity, we look likely to concede at any given moment, and less likely to score than a eunuch at a swingers' party.

If we don't get our skates on and find someone soon we run the risk of burning through our December fixtures without a manager or a credible plan in place. Thankfully, despite receiving well over a hundred CVs plus countless unsolicited calls and texts, it's been far easier to work out the genuine contenders from the time wasters than I had at first feared.

My favourite submissions include a coach looking to step up from a successful career in the under-10s game and a guy with no football experience at all. He backed up a threadbare CV with a selection of oddly staged photos of himself wearing a fancy suit with a Premier League dugout clumsily photoshopped behind him. I also had a man call me claiming to be Sam Allardyce, although I was immediately sceptical. Firstly, he sounded very different from how Sam Allardyce normally sounds on TV, but the main giveaway was that when we asked him to send over a CV he spelt his name incorrectly four times. Ironically, the Sam Allardice who got in touch with us claimed one of his best qualities was attention to detail.

Excitingly, we've also received an application from a serial winner at both non-league and EFL level. He's won countless cups as well as achieving promotion from League One, League Two and the Vanarama National League. He would have been the perfect candidate if all of his achievements hadn't been made on *Football Manager*. Our fifteen-year-old candidate's belief that he's ready to make the jump from his bedroom to IRL will sadly never be put to the test.

We've also received a CV from someone with a huge amount of experience in both our league and several divisions above. He was at Bury FC and Doncaster as well as being at Alfreton for three successful seasons in the Vanarama North. He was my top pick from all the applications until Robbo pointed out that in very small print at the bottom of the document he had specified his job titles at the clubs. He was a ballboy at Bury, the assistant sponge man (whatever that is) at Doncaster and a spectator at Alfreton.

Last and most definitely least, Flash got in touch to put forward a potential candidate. Himself. He said that 'being an agent isn't all it's cracked up to be' and that 'people had stopped taking his calls'. I reminded him that only a few weeks ago he told me he had 'the best job in the world'. He replied by saying 'that nothing in life is permanent'. Sadly I'm start-ing to fear Flash's involvement in my life *is* becoming permanent. He promised me he'd be 'the best manager we've ever had'. I can't fault his self-belief but sadly I can fault almost everything else about him. He's never played, never coached, and I can't even be sure if he's ever watched a game of football. I told him I'd bear him in mind and I'd get in touch if we didn't find anyone with more experience.

After a painful day sifting through all the submissions we've managed to narrow our shortlist down to just three potential candidates, all of whom have been invited for an interview today. One of our contenders pulled out of the race this morn-ing so we are already down to the last two. I'm sadly stuck in London and so will have to settle for a follow-up chat with each candidate on the phone, with Dad, Angie and Robbo conducting the in-person questioning. I'm gutted not to be able to make it but our need for speed outweighs our need for someone with no footballing experience to lead the interviewing process.

Both of our potentials are really exciting and good options for the club for different reasons. Our first interview is with Jim Finnegan. He's a safe and trusted pair of hands who knows the league like the back of those hands. Helpfully, he also knows a decent number of our players from when he was manager of one of our local rivals just a few years ago. He's a recommendation of Tony's, who has described him as 'a proper football man'. I'd say he's probably the favourite for the job.

Our second meeting is with Mike Clegg. At thirty-six he's much younger and very new to the league. He has, however, already impressed us at the start of the season when his battling Atherton Collieries team visited Hurst Cross on the first day of the season. He's had plenty of success with his current club, having won three promotions in five seasons as well as several league and county cups.

After a couple of hours of eager waiting in my theatre dressing room, Dad calls straight after meeting Jim to say that we've found our man.

I give Jim a call.

He seems like a solid enough candidate and definitely knows his stuff. He's a no-nonsense kind of guy and I can certainly see that would appeal to Dad. He's not fond of building from the back and is of the opinion that the team need to 'go back to basics'. In many ways he's a sensible choice, having been there, done that and got several T-shirts in the process. He's friends with Tony, Larry and several other people connected with the club so he'd certainly be a popular appointment and would no doubt get our old guard and our very old guard back onside. He's also been to watch a lot of our games this season and picked up on the fact that we need to be fitter and better organized.

Despite the arguments for moving forward, I'm not totally won over. Our conversation is a little stilted, but then to be fair everything I'm saying is from a tick list I found on askjeeves.com so I'm probably more to blame than him. No matter how hard Jim tries to chat naturally I stick rigidly to my pre-determined prompts. He talks about his previous relationship with our players and I robotically ask him, 'What is your playing philosophy?' He gives his opinion on some of our matches and I ask him, 'How would you instil and build a winning culture at our club?' To be honest, it's remarkable that he's still interested in the job by the time our phone call is over. I don't think I could hand on heart say I'd want to work with me.

I have a think for a few minutes but I can't make up my mind. I'm not blown away by Jim but I imagine he'll inject enough discipline into the squad to keep us up and get us through the season safely. I curse myself for my lack of clarity before texting Dad and the rest of the board to say I'm happy to go ahead if they are.

Dad then calls an hour or so later to say that this time we've definitely found our man.

I call Mike.

He answers, and after chatting to him for fifteen minutes I'm almost immediately blown away. In fact it's one of the first times in my tenure at the club so far when I've had a strong gut instinct on something. I can sense that he's a fantastic fit with not just the club but the town itself. He's enthusiastic and friendly but also very driven with a clear work ethic. He emails over an entire PowerPoint presentation about his management style, his backroom team and our current squad, going through everything in detail. He talks about how he will set the team up, how he will prepare for each game, and how he analyses the opposition. It's very impressive, and it's evident a lot of thought has gone into his pitch. He's also pragmatic about what we need to do in the next three months to guarantee our survival. He says that ultimately we want to be entertaining and attractive to watch but first of all we need to be horrible and hard to beat. He says that we need to become a team that people don't want to play and turn Hurst Cross into a fortress if we are to get out of our current predicament.

'The truth is,' he tells me bluntly, 'at the moment everybody wants to play against you. Every manager knows that if you turn up and put a proper shift in, you'll win. You've got too many in the team who don't graft hard enough.'

I'm briefly fretful that we're going to need another squad overhaul, but Mike says that's not necessarily the case. 'You need a couple in there with some legs, but really you've got one of the best squads in the league. We just need to motivate them.'

I'm surprised by how easy it is to chat to Mike. In a world where I've sometimes felt like I'm not too sure what to say, I find myself having an honest and free-flowing conversation. I'm not trying to hide my lack of inside knowledge nor am I holding back on giving my opinion. I discard my cue cards and just open up about the experience so far. How painful so much of the season has been and, at times, how overwhelming.

We end up chatting for almost two hours about this season and also about the future, what we want to build.

When we end the call, for the first time in a while I feel positive, and certainly less terrified.

I speak to Dad and very quickly both he and the rest of the board agree unanimously. We've found our man.

And just like that there is once again a sense of hope. With just over a third of the season played, maybe this is the moment when everything will click into place.

Maybe this is the moment when I'll start to feel like I know what I'm doing.

Maybe . . .

15

Final Throw of the Dice?

It's the first Saturday of December and I'm driving down the M3 to Bashley FC to watch us in Mike's first game in charge, a week later than scheduled. We were supposed to play at home last week but the match was postponed. Over a third of the pitch remains stubbornly frozen. The shadow of Sid Sykes (whoever he is, or was), or more accurately his stand, looms large over the ground, creating a sizeable patch of earth that's blocked from the morning sun. It's preventing the earth from thawing so the pitch has remained rock hard. There have been several different attempts to melt the ice using increasingly avant-garde methods. These include covering the pitch in doormats, hiring a large gas torch, blowing the grass with a series of hairdryers, and placing a large propane heater under a plastic tarpaulin. Not only did none of these work, but the latter could have easily started a large-scale fire and burnt my uncle alive when he decided to climb under the plastic sheeting to, quote, 'check everything was working'. It was a wasted week, but at least we're able to say we've given the whole pitch the hairdryer treatment as well as the players.

I'm trepidatious, but for the first time since the start of the season I'm also genuinely excited. I know it's still going to be tough – our opponents are in the play-off spots and will fancy their chances – but I feel hopeful. I head down the motorway, driving through the drizzle, with a sense of belief that we'll see an improved performance today. It's been an eventful week and it feels like lots of progress has been made.

Our supporters are delighted with the new manager and there's been a buzz across our Twitter all week. Even @TheAnonymousRobin has led the charge in celebrating what has widely been viewed as a sound appointment. A few people on the unofficial official fans' forum have gone so far as to say the club has made a good decision! We've even had positive coverage in the non-league weekly paper which earlier in the year had named Mike as one of the top twenty non-league managers of the decade.

We've also got all our balls back so we'll be well stocked for our next home game. I asked Deano how we managed to get them. His response was simply, 'There's some things it's best you don't know.'

Behind the scenes Mike has been a total breath of fresh air and seems to have had an immediate impact on everyone at the club. He already knows each volunteer by name and has had four training sessions with the squad over the fortnight. He made a big impression on them and has reached out to each player individually to get their take on the season so far. He's also had more of a heart-to-heart with a couple of them, including the increasingly downcast Boothy, who's not scored since our mauling at the hands of Spennymoor over two months ago and has fallen out of the starting eleven. Mike says he's 'a top fella' who just needs 'some love' and is determined to help him end his now over 900-minute goal drought.

I've spoken to Mike every other day and it feels like we have a clear plan, the first part of which is to get as many league points as possible before the new year. We've brought in two new players already who, Dad and I have been promised, will run through walls for the club. The first is a hard-tackling box-to-box midfielder called Michael Brewster, and the second is a skilful winger called Ben Hardcastle, both of whom have followed Mike across from Atherton. Ben was under contract and we've had to agree a transfer fee of £1,000 for his services while Michael has signed a contract with us until the end of the season. We're hoping to add a new keeper and another striker to our ranks by the start of next week too. We've found negotiations with clubs tricky as our 'spend first and ask reasonable questions later' pre-season strategy has meant everyone is demanding well over the odds for any player we're interested in. Every player we contact also wants a full contract as they know everyone else at the club is on one. We've sadly made an expensive rod for our own backs that we're going to have to put up with until next season.

It's 1.30 and I'm still just under an hour away from the ground. The traffic and the rain are starting to get heavier so I give Mike a quick call on hands-free to check he and the rest of the squad have arrived and everything is all right.

'Hello, mate,' I say.

'Hello, Chairman,' he replies jovially.

'Just checking you've got to the ground OK?'

'All good, we're here and ready.'

'Horrible weather,' I add.

'Dead sunny here, pal,' he responds.

We go over the starting eleven and there are a few changes from our last defeat. Both Ben and Michael are going straight into the starting line-up while captain Jono is dropped to the bench. We've changed the formation too, setting up more defensively with a packed midfield of five and four at the back. Boothy has also done enough in training to get the nod and lead the line up front on his own. The hope being that once he breaks his duck the goals will flow like bargain-priced wine over Christmas.

'The aim today is to keep it tight and not get beat in the first twenty minutes,' Mike explains with reassuring determination. 'Get points on the board and start to pull away.'

We chat for a little longer before I wish him all the best for the big game ahead. We're yet to meet in person and I'm looking forward to having a proper debrief post-match, hopefully with at least an extra point under our belt.

The rain starts to hammer down on the roof of the car. A couple of wrong turns and a steadily building tailback means I'm now in danger of being late. It's just after 2.30 and I'm still at least half an hour away from the ground. I start to panic about missing kick-off when Dad calls to talk about the game and give his predictions.

'It's a tricky game,' Dad says, managing his own expectations as much as mine.

'I know.'

'I just want to see a bit of fight today,' he adds.

'Me too. I'd take a draw now if I could,' I admit.

'You there yet?' asks Dad.

'Not yet,' I reply.

'I'm five minutes away,' he adds. 'I'm hoping this sunny weather's a sign.'

With that, Dad warns me about the lack of parking at the ground and hangs up. I'm left waiting anxiously to get to the match, my nerves starting to ramp up as kick-off approaches with the car only creeping forward. Eventually, at a little after 3 p.m., I arrive in the lush surrounds of the Glen Mex Stadium.

Immediately something doesn't feel right. The weather's still terrible and there's ample parking. In fact the car park is basically empty, and as I make my way to the turnstiles there's an alarming quiet in the air considering the match is five minutes in. There's no smell of pre-match food, no advertisements for the game and, most importantly, no spectators to be seen.

I feel the blood rush to my head and my heart fall through my stomach as I realize I've made a dreadful mistake. I take my phone from my pocket and cack-handedly scroll through for confirmation of my fears. We're playing Basford United, not Bashley. I've gone to the wrong club and to the wrong end of the country. I've driven two and a half hours down to the Hampshire coast to watch a Northern Premier League football match. I curse myself and my geographic ineptitude out loud before running back to the car, fleeing from the elements.

I frantically look up the journey to Basford to see if there's any way of making the second half but I know it's futile. I paw through Google Maps and see that the nearest major city to me is Southampton. I'm 211 miles from where I'm supposed to be, in the suburbs of Nottingham.

I've already missed the first ten minutes so I try to listen to the live commentary on my phone. The Wi-Fi from the car is awful so it's hard to follow exactly what's happening, but I'm relieved to discover the score is still 0–0. I do my best to try to warm up and dry off as I hunker down to support the team in the only way now available to me.

There's not much for our commentary team to talk about other than a couple of half chances early on, and a dull first half ends goalless with neither side creating anything clear-cut. Despite the lack of entertainment from inside my car, and by the sound of it on the terraces, I'm delighted. There's been no comical early catastrophe nor has there been a lapse of concentration just before the break. We've shut out credible opposition and we're still in the mix going into the second half.

Feeling somewhat soothed, I decide to use half-time to get a head start on the long journey home. I go to start my car but I'm dealt another severe blow: it's electric, and completely out of battery. I'm stranded in the middle of nowhere, unable to watch the team and now unable to get home too. I punch my steering wheel in anger, accidentally setting off the alarm. I flap about trying to make it stop, to no avail.

After a few minutes of panicking I'm interrupted by a gentle knock on the window from a white-haired man in a Bashley tracksuit. He has a kindly face with a small grey moustache. I'm guessing he's their groundsman.

'Everything OK, young man?' he enquires.

'I'm fine,' I say, desperate for the conversation to end before it's even begun, the alarm still crying into the miserable afternoon.

'The match has been postponed due to the rain,' he offers with a sympathetic expression.

I go to explain the situation but in the end think better of it and thank him for letting me know.

'You a Bashy fan then?' he asks amiably.

'Oh, yeah,' I respond unsurely.

'I don't think I've seen you before. You come to a lot of the matches then?'

'Erm, no,' I say, faltering. 'This would have been my first match.'

'So how are you a Bashy supporter then?' he asks, confused, his eyes narrowing a little underneath his quizzical bushy bashy eyebrows.

'I've just supported from a distance,' I say feebly.

There's an awkward pause that's exacerbated when the car alarm abruptly stops, leaving us both staring at each other in a silence underscored only by the rough wind and littoral rain.

'I'll leave you to it,' he says finally, writing me off as a nut job and heading back into the ground. Just before he's out of sight he turns back and shouts, 'Maybe see you at the next match?'

'No!' I reply, winding my window back up.

I swipe through my phone and start the commentary again. I've missed the first few minutes of the second half but the deadlock is yet to be broken. The game sounds less cagey though and more open. Basford are surging forward continually but we're holding on and, for the first time in a long while, defending resolutely.

I let out a cry as Ben Hardcastle breaks free only to have his shot cleared off the line. We're sticking to our game plan as we near the hour mark. It doesn't sound pretty but we're managing to contain our opposition and carve out a few decent chances of our own too.

Just when it's starting to feel like we're making inroads, all is lost as Basford take the lead. We're caught napping at the back and their striker is able to put the ball away after being left unmarked in the six-yard box. I try to maintain my bullish mindset but, like my journey, things go south very quickly when the hosts double the lead ten minutes later through a powerful strike that Tarantula can only push into the back of his own net. I fall forward on to my steering wheel, triggering the car alarm again as a familiar wave of match-day angst washes over me.

As I teeter on the edge of despair I'm reminded that we're in a new era. The car alarm once again desists, and just minutes later we've pulled one back. Our top scorer Josh Wilson bangs in his fifth penalty of the season and his ninth goal in total. I clench my fist as I cling on to the faint hope that the team can leave Nottingham (and I Hampshire) with at least a point for our efforts.

The signs aren't good though, and Basford raise their level substantially. We're stuck on the back foot for the next ten minutes with only Tarantula to thank for keeping us in the game. Then, as our volunteer commentator pleads for our ever-retreating defence to push up the pitch, a clever through ball finds their forward who puts the game to bed, making the score 3–1.

To our credit, our heads don't go down and we carry on fighting. We pump the ball long, and after a series of free kicks manage to score from a corner on ninety minutes. We continue to huff and puff through six minutes of injury time but we're unable to blow the house down and the game ends 3–2. It's our fifth consecutive loss and our thirteenth of the season.

We might have improved, but it's not enough. We've still only won four in the league all season, we're out of every cup, and we've finally slipped back into the bottom three again. Mike has got an almighty job on his hands.

A text comes through from Dad: *Where are you?*

I put my phone in the glove compartment, slide back my car seat and wait for the AA to rescue me.

Part Three

16

Now or Never

My grandmother died on 13 December and the funeral took place a little under a month later. She was cremated on a Friday at Dukinfield Crematorium with the wake held at the club later that afternoon. Ironically the atmosphere was more jovial than it usually is after a match. Her passing came as a horrible shock to all of our family and it's put the last few weeks into perspective. The game feels like life and death until someone dies and then it feels like a game again.

We're now eight games without a win and have taken just a single point from six league fixtures. We're second bottom and six points from safety. Things are starting to get desperate.

After our match against Basford, we went on to lose 2–1 to FC United of Manchester. Despite being at home our 180 or so supporters were totally outnumbered by over a thousand FC fans who took over the ground for the day. It looked like an eighty-eighth-minute equalizer would be enough to earn us a point until our fragile hearts were broken by a last-second Michael Donohue winner, sending us into Christmas without any comfort and absolutely no joy. The mood was so despondent post-match that it was suggested by a group of our supporters that we might be cursed. After a couple of drinks I found myself seriously entertaining the idea of asking a local priest to visit and carry out a late-night exorcism on the pitch.

We lost our first home game of 2020 to league leaders South Shields and the only glimmer of hope since our win at Buxton two and a half months ago has been a goalless draw away at Stalybridge Celtic on a Baltic New Year's Day. It was a physical game of few chances played on a bobbly pitch. Both teams were lacking in creativity and confidence and, although we had a glorious opportunity to win it late on, a draw was a fair result. Who knows, perhaps if we'd got the priest in things might've been different.

Today, just one day after saying goodbye to my grandma, I'm back at Hurst Cross with my entire family for our match against Stafford Rangers. We're drained and emotionally raw and hoping that after a tough week we can be briefly transported from our grief. A win would at the very least give us all something to smile about even if it's just for the evening.

'I'm not coming again if they lose,' Mum half jokes.

'I won't either way,' adds Dad glibly.

We all laugh, and I'm reminded of how much I used to enjoy football and of its unique power to bring people together, lifting the doom in a way few things can.

If we're finally going to end our most recent winless run then today is undoubtedly our best chance. Stafford are the only club below us in the league. If we lose and results don't go our way we could find ourselves nine points adrift, but if we win it could be the catalyst we've been crying out for.

We need goals, and we need them yesterday. Mike, or Cleggy as he's affectionately known, has managed to bring in two new strikers and it feels like a last chance saloon. Our budget has been stretched, ripped, patched up and stretched again but both Dad and I are determined to back our new manager to the hilt.

The match starts, and it's everything I'd imagined – full of industry and fight, but devoid of any kind of quality. Both teams hack the ball out of their own halves as the tackles fly in. After the first fifteen it's the away side who've had the better of the chances and we've got our new keeper Greg Hartley to thank for a couple of smart saves, keeping the score at 0–0.

Despite the importance of the match I feel terribly flat, and the supporters seem subdued too. After half a season of being served complete sporting dross or last-minute trauma there's little to cheer about and we all desperately need the team to give us a lift. Nerves are getting the better of us and despite our huffing and puffing the house of Stafford looks very secure. We've all been conditioned to assume the worst, and that inevitability is confirmed after twenty-seven minutes when Stafford Rangers take the lead through a Josh Green free kick. The rippling of the net is met with a ghostly hush and there's a catching murmur that spreads through the crowd like flu as the supporters start to face up to a successive relegation.

Tom, ever the optimist, tries to put a positive spin on our situation. 'There's an upside to going down,' he says with faux merriment, throwing his arm around me. 'I've never been to Bootle for example.'

'There's still hope,' offers his daughter Bethany defiantly from under her brolly.

I appreciate them trying to raise my spirits but I feel awful, and so does everyone else. The majority of our supporters stand idly behind the goal, hunched over on the terraces or wrapped up in thick anoraks taking refuge in the Sid Sykes Stand. Even the usually ebullient Stella doesn't have it in her to bang her drum. We're out of fight and out of hope, and judging from how we're playing so are the squad. On thirty-nine minutes Josh Wilson has a deflected shot sail over the bar but that's it for the first half. The supporters shuffle off to the bar like a confusion of hungry wildebeest plodding through the Serengeti.

I stay outside and circle the ground like a zombie. After months of trying to put a brave face on the situation, I'm done. It's clear we're going down and there's nothing I can do but watch. Why did I think I could do this? I've tried to force my way into a world I don't belong in and I've been caught out. I think about next season morosely and wonder if the league below will prove just as unforgiving as the one we're in now.

'You've killed the club,' scolds the voice in my head.

Beaten by the cold, I head into the directors' lounge where the Stafford Rangers bosses are in fine fettle. They sip their tea loudly, smacking their lips in anticipation of a possible three points. One of them remarks that 'the great escape is on' while another protests that 'they're too good to go down'. I want to punch them both in the mouth but instead I offer them a Rich Tea biscuit and a refill. Our directors and volunteers, meanwhile, sit in sombre contemplation, looking down the double-barrelled gun of relegation. Reginald's kindly face is careworn while Angie and Robbo look like they've each done ten rounds with Tyson Fury. Dad stands outside on the decking with Mum looking out on to the divot-strewn pitch praying for a miracle. Grandad sits beside them on a picnic table sipping impossibly sweet coffee from his thermos flask. He's just lost his wife and to have brought him here feels cruel.

We've had so many moments in the season masquerading as rock bottom. From as far back as the last-minute defeat to Bamber to our last-second loss against FC United of Manchester, there have been so many times when it's felt like it wasn't possible for things to get any worse, but this feels different. If the score stays the same we'll be rooted to the foot of the table with an Everest-size mountain to climb. There are forty-five minutes left to decide our fate.

The players return, and the stadium gradually repopulates with pensive faces and bodies double-dipped in many layers, each gloved hand clutching a polystyrene cup of Bovril and every neck protected by the thickest of scarves. Thunder rumbles overhead and the skies darken. The wind is bracing and the cold cuts right through you. Despite the elements the eleven on the pitch look focused, their chests puffed out in readiness. It's clear words have been had at half-time. It's now or never, do or die.

We kick off and we're certainly not flat any more. We contest every fifty-fifty, and we're first to every second ball. Most importantly, with the wind in our favour we're going long and direct. It's not pretty but in these conditions it's effective. The ball gets caught in the air, and as we press it's almost impossible for Stafford to get a moment's respite. Our captain, Michael Brewster, screams at the lads to 'keep going' as we pepper their goal with crosses and long diagonals. After the first ten minutes of the second half the score is the same but their keeper has made a catalogue of brilliant saves.

Cleggy prowls the touchline, applauding and motivating as we probe for the equalizer. As the minutes race by we win a free kick 30 yards or so from goal. The ball is floated awkwardly into their box, and after an hour of keeping us at bay we finally break their resolve. Josh Wilson leaps like a gazelle to nod the ball past their stranded keeper. The supporters behind the goal erupt and we all celebrate wildly, hugging and high-fiving with ferocity. It's probably the most important goal we've scored all season and suddenly Hurst Cross is pumping with energy. It's a game we can't afford to lose but it's also one we can't draw either. We need the victory today and we all play our part in roaring the team forward in search of another goal. We have thirty minutes left to save our season and everyone knows it.

The ball is pumped forward again and again but, like those guys in the 118 ads, Stafford have got our number. Each long ball is headed back or cleared away as the clock ticks down. The rain has been falling consistently for at least an hour and the middle of the pitch is like porridge, making it impossible to pass the ball. For a neutral it can't be good to watch but for anyone with skin in the game it's nerve-shredding viewing.

Dad is lost in the game, unable or unwilling to speak, and we stand together, waiting in football purgatory to see whether we are destined for heaven or hell. My mum screams passionately as the ball rolls out for a throw-in.

'Be better!' she shouts. 'Just be much better!'

Grandad watches on, poker-faced, calmly emptying out the

dregs of his flask. 'There's time,' he says with a confidence ill-suited to the season we've had.

'Not much time,' Dad whispers to me with trepidation in his voice and bags under his eyes.

The minutes are slipping away, but out of nowhere we manage to create an opportunity. Our winger Ben Hardcastle goes on a mazy run, gliding across the boggy earth before whipping in a low and dangerous cross. The Stafford full-back tries to clear but the ball cannons off his own midfielder and bounces back into the fray. There's a flurry of chaos and it's almost impossible to see the ball for bodies falling and diving around the six-yard box. Then suddenly our hearts are in our mouths. The ball rolls across to Shezza, who's waiting unmarked at the back post. It looks like a certain goal, but before he can get his foot to it the ball stops dead in the mud and one of their defenders is able to clear. Gasps of incredulity echo through the frozen air.

It looks like it's going to end in the same way I've seen so many of our matches end this season. We've dominated but we just can't convert our chances. It's not over yet but there's certainly a woman of ample size warming up somewhere.

Then, with our season hanging by the thinnest of threads, the ball rolls out for a corner. Dad and I watch helplessly, hoping that this might be the moment when our luck finally changes.

Ben Hardcastle runs over to take it. He wipes his brow and takes a short run-up before delivering a looping ball into the box. My heart beats so hard I feel like I've swallowed a nightclub. It floats past their defenders, away from the outstretched arm of their keeper, over our strikers and towards the head of fellow new boy Brewster. He rises like a salmon and the ball whacks him right in the ear. He grimaces as it bobbles off his shoulder, catches his knee, and somehow nestles into the bottom corner. It's one of the clumsiest finishes you'll see in your life but it doesn't matter one bit.

Brewster roars with delight, skidding over the grass on his knees towards the corner flag. His teammates flood towards him in wild celebration. Cleggy goes full Mourinho and belts it down the touchline as our supporters go wild. Angie, Robbo and Reginald trip the light fantastic while Dad and I wave our arms around like we've won the lottery. Mum embraces Grandad, and Grandad embraces the occasion as the noise from the ground reverberates around the whole of Surrey Street.

'Told you there was time,' he says, flashing a sage smile.

The celebrations are soon put on ice though. The fourth official indicates a stonking six minutes of added time, an announcement greeted with befuddled rancour as the Hurst Cross faithful brace themselves for a buttock-clenching finish.

I can't take it and flee to the bar. I sit thoughtfully, head bowed, rubbing my temples while counting the minutes on my phone. I plead softly for the deliverance of the final whistle but instead hear the muffled groan of the crowd and dart back outside. I'm greeted by my worst nightmare: their striker lies face down in the box as our players crowd around the referee, furiously remonstrating. It can't be, I think to myself.

'It's a bloody dive!' screams Angie.

'He didn't touch him!' pleads Dad indignantly.

The referee runs over to the linesman and the two officials lock themselves in consultation. The crowd boo and hiss as we wait with bated breath for confirmation of the inevitable. After what feels like an eternity the ref runs back, pointing dramatically. It's a goal kick! My knees almost buckle as the ball is thumped back into the safety of their half.

Dad looks ashen as we cling on for dear life – just two minutes left now. They have a header cleared off the line. I throw up in my mouth a little and swallow it back down.

'You've got to learn to enjoy it,' says one of our supporters compassionately.

'Do you enjoy it?' I ask.

'Of course not. I've been coming here for twenty-five years,' he responds irritably.

The ball is clubbed back into our box and headed out for a corner. The Stafford keeper runs up to join the fray. We must be into the final seconds now. I close my eyes and listen quietly to the dull thump of the ball being propelled into the box and the desperate clamour of our supporters. There's a series of headers and shouts before the referee's whistle cuts through the commotion. It's over!

Cleggy raises his fists victoriously as he and his staff head over to the home faithful to applaud their support. The players follow closely behind as a reinvigorated Stella beats her drum, leading the fans into a spontaneous rendition of 'We are staying up!' It's unquestionably a downgrading on the ambitions from the start of the season but at least it feels like everyone is pulling in the same direction. The players head towards the tunnel, their knees wet and grass-stained and their faces spattered with dirt. As they exit they're met with vociferous and boisterous applause. Even Larry and Frank Taunton call out 'well played' as the squad make their way into the changing room like heroes returning from battle.

We've been at the club for almost nine months now and for the first time since we arrived there's a sense of genuine joy around the place. We've still got a lot of work to do but at least for tonight we can enjoy ourselves.

The crowd buoyantly head off to celebrate the long-forgotten taste of victory. I watch them slip away through the gates and out into the lamplit street. I run out on to the pitch, holding my arms skyward and craning my neck backwards, the icy air rushing through my lungs. My face is hot with tears and I find myself, not for the first time, sobbing at the end of a match. This is different though: it's not tears of self-pity or of bitter disappointment, it's just an outpouring of emotion. I'm crying from grief, relief and joy all at the same time. I applaud and punch the air repeatedly as my body pulses with adrenalin. Suddenly I feel arms lock around the back of me and as I turn I'm confronted by the grinning face of our goalkeeper coach Killian.

'Come on!' he screams in jubilation.

He scoops me into the air, spinning me round like a rag doll before landing me clumsily with a thump.

Larry, Frank and Reginald prop up the bar while Robbo, Angie and Deano split a bottle of red wine in the corner. Dale, Georgina and Simon watch on with delight, and Mum, Dad and Grandad sit together and raise their glasses to their late mother and wife. Stella, already four sheets to the wind, bangs merrily on her drum. Even the kitmen kick back and let loose.

When the players arrive clutching trays full of chips and chilli, each one is greeted with a cheer as they take their seat. Round after round is bought as conversation turns to song. Tom and Bethany fire up the jukebox and soon everyone is on their feet dancing. We've got a week before our next match and for the first time in a long time we'll all be able to enjoy the weekend.

At about 1 a.m. I stumble out on to Surrey Street with Lucy, my head already pounding in preparation for the morning. We drunkenly slide into an Uber and head off, the lights of the bar illuminating the early morning and the sound of merriment echoing through the street.

17

Can't Stop Us Now

We're sat in a high-end tapas restaurant in Manchester city centre. The tables are made from upcycled oak and the lighting is moody and atmospheric. The man behind the bar looks like a grey-haired Juan Mata. Since the place is reportedly owned by the Manchester United midfielder it could well be him.

We thumb through the menu, waiting for our drinks to arrive. Dad reclines comfortably in his chair while Mike, his wife Sam, Mike's assistant Healdy and his partner Claire chat merrily. Deano, Dale, Angie and Robbo share stories they've no doubt told countless times before.

It's been a fantastic couple of months that have seen us lose only one game in ten, notching up six wins and three draws along the way. Since the start of the year we've only lost twice and have picked up an incredible twenty-two points. In our first five months we only managed fifteen. And it's not just the results that have been impressive, it's the complete change in mindset. We've gone from looking under-confident and unfit to believing we can win every game and outrun anyone in the league.

We followed our dramatic last-minute win against Stafford with a superb victory over Morpeth Town where, after going 1–0 down, we found our shooting boots and ended up winning 4–1. The equalizer from Shezza was a piledriver from 35 yards out and worth the three points alone. With confidence building we picked up a hard-won point at Radcliffe Borough thanks to Liam Tomsett's first of the season before battling to a 1–0 home win against Lancaster. It got a little tense towards the end but the result meant we dragged ourselves out of the relegation zone for the first time since early December last year.

Although a 3–1 away defeat in our next match against Scarborough reminded us of our fallibility, we were able to bounce back at home against Witton Albion. It was a great occasion watched by a bumper crowd, among them several of our junior teams as mascots, and included a goal from Boothy. His first in over eighteen weeks!

We then drew 1–1 away at Whitby before holding high-flying Warrington by the same score at our place. Finally, five goals in two games from our top scorer Josh Wilson helped us to consecutive home wins against tough opposition. We first got our revenge over Scarborough, beating them 2–0, before again coming from behind to win 3–1 against Mickleover on a cold Tuesday night. After being seen by many for so much of the season as a soft touch, we're fast getting a reputation for our never-say-die attitude. Josh has also cemented himself as our top scorer despite playing almost half of the matches in central defence. He's managed to bag eighteen goals, with eleven of them coming from the penalty spot.

Apart from the loss in early January to runaway leaders

South Shields we're unbeaten at home in 2020, and based on the last ten games we're top of the league form table! More importantly, recent results have moved us up comfortably into the middle of the actual table, meaning we can start to relax and plan for next season. I've hardly had any panic attacks lately and after months of anxiety I was actually able to enjoy watching us in a competitive match for the first time ever against Mickleover. Even when we were losing I didn't once think about hiding in the storage unit, and I even saw Dad smile at one point.

It's not just the men's first team that's on the up. The whole club has been lifted. The junior teams are attending matches at Hurst Cross more frequently, the bar sales are up, and the women's first team are also improving after a dip in form. In our inaugural season AUFC are on track to finish in a respectable mid-table position in the Greater Manchester Women's Football League first division.

Our overall attendance is on the rise, smiles are on faces, and even the most pessimistic at the club agree we've turned a corner. Although it's unlikely, if our form continues we could force ourselves into play-off contention. At full time on Tuesday there were even a few chants of 'We are going up!' and 'Michael Clegg's barmy army!'

It's made me realize something about running a football club. So much of what I do, what we do, is often irrelevant. As soon as results started to go our way everyone was happier and nobody was in the slightest bit interested in John Smith's or what shade of red the terraces are painted. It's a business like no other, where the amount of work done by those who own or run a club doesn't really make a huge amount of difference to its stakeholders, the supporters. We could improve the facilities, transform our finances and grow the club for the future, but we'd be judged entirely on the one thing we have no control over at all – how we are performing on the pitch. It creates a constant feeling of being lost at sea, that no matter how hard you swim you're always at the mercy of the tide.

So with that in mind we've taken our new manager and his assistant out for dinner with their partners to say thank you for calming the waters and mooring our sanity over the last three months.

Cleggy's incredibly excited about the future. He thinks we can challenge for promotion next year and doesn't want to rule out our chances of making the play-offs this season. Time isn't on our side but football is a funny game and he says 'stranger things have happened'.

I just want to make sure we cross the line to mathematical safety as soon as possible. It's not been a good season but as long as it's not an unmitigated disaster I can live with that. I've done a bit of back-of-a-cigarette-pack maths and we probably need three more wins to definitively say we're safe. I'm determined to make sure we learn our lessons from this season and move on. Sensible spending, no more over-inflated contracts, and a suitable amount of socks for starters. Above all, we won't get carried away in 2020/21. We'll keep our feet on the ground and remember how much of a slog this season has been.

'There's so much potential for the club,' enthuses Mike.

'Totally,' agrees Healdy.

Our drinks arrive, and as the Rioja starts to flow so too do our imaginations as Mike and his deputy set out their vision for next season. They say that much of how we've played since they arrived has been pragmatic, a belts-and-braces approach to ensure we stopped the rot and stayed up. Now that's almost achieved we can start to look forward.

'We want to outwork teams, but it's got to be good to watch,' Mike says passionately.

We start talking through potential transfer targets and players who we think will want to join. We want to be ambitious but we also need to push the wage bill down. There's no way we can continue to spend at the same rate as this season.

'We got carried away this season,' says Dad, stating the obvious.

Mike says that we're going to need to bide our time, that we've got a bit of a reputation for paying over the odds, so we're going to have to hold our nerve and accept that we might lose out on a few players initially.

'We need to make it clear the club's not an open cheque book,' he states.

'At the moment I think a lot of lads think you're a bit naive,' Healdy observes. 'Good guys but not really business savvy.'

I nod, Dad seethes.

'We also want to come up with a proper recruitment plan,' Mike continues. 'Be wary of agents saying they can solve your problems. There's a guy who calls himself Flash who you should avoid like the plague.'

We talk more and find ourselves explaining how we became co-chairmen and the family link we have with the club.

'It was all Jonathan's idea,' Dad jokes. 'He said it would bring us closer together. I was a happy man before Ashton United!'

We all laugh, and I quietly wonder how large the kernel of truth is in what Dad's just said. Over the last year it's definitely true to say we've spent more time together but it's probably brought us closer to killing each other than anything else.

A cavalcade of delicious and colourful food arrives presented in fancy granite pots and plates. As we tuck in, Mike and Healdy ask us more about what we want to achieve and what our long-term plans are at the club.

'What does success look like?' asks Healdy.

Dad and I both fall silent for a moment and think. I feel a bit silly because it's not something I've thought about that much. As daft as it might sound there's never been the time to get ahead of the game and come up with an actionable plan.

In non-league you're constantly trying to balance your 'real job and life' with your club responsibilities, which are, to all intents and purposes, another job and another life all at once. Whether you're a club secretary, kitman, sponge man (still not sure what that is), groundsperson or an owner/chairman, you're in a job where you're constantly on call and most likely never paid. In fact you probably make a significant net loss in any of the above roles, especially mine! It's almost impossible to feel like you're on top of anything; in fact you'll most likely feel you're always behind, desperately trying to catch up with the rest of the pack.

Running a football club hasn't been anything like I thought it would be. I'd foolishly imagined it would be a chance to reconnect with home while allowing myself a glimpse into a world I've always yearned to be part of. The truth is that for the most part it's been like being stuck in a washing machine running on turbo drive with my hands tied behind my back.

Since our very first day pulling up in the car park of Lionel's Lino Emporium we've been blindsided at every step. Whether it be unearthing debts, dealing with disastrous results and urgent building repairs, or wading through a litany of rules and regulations just to maintain what already exists, we've spent most of our time locked in a vicious circle of putting out fires and reacting to problems. Each week there's been a tumult of issues that have needed to be dealt with, and that's made setting our own agenda impossible.

It's taken me almost a year to realize that my job is to remove myself from the emotion of the game rather than get lost in weekly worry every time we don't win or when something goes wrong. I've made so much of the season about me and how terrible I've felt when results haven't gone our way, when I need to be one of the few people who are able to look past a handful of defeats and keep us on track behind the scenes. I might not be able to enjoy it but I need to be able to stomach it – or as Cleggy puts it, 'don't get too high off the highs, or too low from the lows'.

We all huddle over a napkin and, surrounded by patatas bravas, Padrón peppers and half-tucked-into paella, write down a blueprint made up of eight major goals that will act as lodestars for how we make decisions for the club both on and off the pitch.

1. We want to make sure the club's identity reflects the town it's in – hard-working and honest. (We only want to have players who really want to play for us.)
2. We want to attract young, hungry players who have the potential to make the move into professional football.

3. We want to make sure that the club is progressive, with a one-club mentality. This means having a competitive, fully funded women's set-up established in the next three years and ensuring all our junior teams and academies are fully connected to our senior squads.
4. We want to grow our fan base both in real life and online – this means attracting new people to the club!
5. We want to improve the facilities at the club – the pitch, the ground, and where we train.
6. We want to get promoted back into the Vanarama North (or whatever that league may be called by the time we're there!).
7. We want to make sure we are a club that plays an essential role within the community, delivering courses to schools, engaging in community events.
8. We want all this to be fun, or at the very least bearable.

I won't lie, it feels exciting. On top of the good results, it genuinely feels like the moment I've been waiting for. The time when everything clicks together and at long last we can all start to enjoy the experience and look forward to match days rather than fearing them.

More food and wine arrives. Bottles are popped open, toasts are made and promises given in increasingly slurred words. We chat, we laugh, and have a brilliant night.

Our current form is nothing short of sensational, and with two months of the season left to play things could get even better.

We raise our glasses to the future.

Nothing can stop us now.

18

Stoppage Time

Football was suspended nationwide on 13 March 2020, and not long after that the league declared the season null and void. What started as a temporary stoppage was soon confirmed as a permanent halt. Some clubs found themselves the recipients of an unlikely reprieve while others lost out on almost certain promotion. It was a tumultuous time full of uncertainty, endless Zoom meetings and a failed legal bid from South Shields. The champions in waiting were twelve points clear having played thirty-three games and were bitterly unlucky to be denied their crown and place in the National League North.

We ended up in seventeenth, having played twenty-nine games in total. With thirteen left to play we were seven points clear of the drop and eighteen points shy of the play-offs. We'd crashed out of all the cups, both local and national, meaning our season was most likely all but over, although with five games in hand there will always be the faintest of question marks hanging like gossamer over that unfinished season. A sentence without a full stop, which will always make a hard-wired optimist like me wonder what might have been.

The ups, the downs, the last-second defeats and the last-minute wins counted for nothing. All that effort and emotion, the successes and the many failures of the last nine months were expunged from the record books. Our defensive mishaps, Shezza's 35-yard stormer and Josh Wilson's countless penalties were converted to relics from a forgotten season that trailed off like ellipses. From a purely technical point of view, history will show that our first season in charge never officially happened, despite a hell of a lot happening.

Stands were shut down, social clubs were shuttered up, and meat pies were left to go stale. Football dissolved into the distance, and as the dust began to settle, clubs were forced to negotiate their way through 'the new normal' – a world full of questions without answers, terraces without supporters and bills without income. It was a hard slog that laid bare the inequalities between grassroots and elite football, and the gap between the haves and the have-nots grew exponentially.

Suddenly hundreds, if not thousands, of volunteers from football's nomadic non-league family found themselves thrown into terrifying new roles. Their responsibilities shifted from running their clubs on a match day to saving their clubs from being run into the ground. Clubs were plunged into the red, forced to focus on furlough rather than football and obsess over business rate relief rather than results on the pitch. For many, they were no longer fighting for promotion or to stay in their league but simply to stay in business.

This book has sought to follow the lighter contours of our beautiful game, but for the longest time they were bitterly

hard to find. Several clubs, including our local rivals Droylsden FC, were forced to close their doors, potentially for ever,
overwhelmed by the Covid pandemic and the constant fog of
unpredictability that shrouded our world. To so many clubs,
much-loved supporters and volunteers were lost, and like
everyone they were unable to grieve properly, forbidden from
saying goodbye.

Slowly but surely, as the world caught up with its new condition, so too did non-league. We found a new purpose and
place within the community, and despite being apart from
each other discovered different ways to connect. The match-
day office was put to use as a food pantry, and instead of
programmes we printed colouring books that Robbo and
Angie posted through letter boxes for families with children.
Our captain Michael Brewster ran online fitness classes for
OAPs, and I ran a Zoom quiz for everyone that started off
being very popular but, like most Zoom quizzes, soon became
very unpopular. When we were finally allowed, we hosted a
huge outdoor event with several local charities that was
attended by over 2,000 people and included a Skillz and Drillz
session by our management and squad, a bouncy castle, ice
cream and, most importantly, a chance to come together and
remind ourselves of what we missed so much.

Larry and Frank Taunton distributed shopping for those
who were shielding, while many of our players worked front-
line jobs. Deano's small team of pitch-maintenance volunteers
grew into an outdoor army of social Samaritans, and Dale
added the role of Covid Officer and food pantry administra-
tor to his mountain of job titles. Our young media volunteers
started a podcast, and Cleggy set up a support network for

players released from professional clubs who were looking at going into non-league. At the age of seventy-eight, our tea lady Mavis took up long-distance running and her grandson Pete took up shouting at her for a change. After a tough first season, Boothy moved on and Josh Wilson made the decision to hang up his boots for good. Jamie Benshaw found a new club, and Flash left the industry and retrained as a hospitality manager.

As for Dad and me, we were pushed back into the routine of reacting rather than acting and any thought of setting our own agenda was quickly abandoned. We focused on steering the club through the pandemic and swam as hard as we could against the tide, managing to keep both ourselves and the club's head just about above water. Fortunately, because we had so many players on contract we were able to furlough a lot of our squad. Those who weren't, we were able to support and we did what we could. We endeavoured to be compassionate and caring and did everything in our power to make sure there would be a club for everyone to come back to. Running a football club without any football taking place was like wine without cheese, Christmas without turkey, or chips without fish, but as a failed vegan I was used to depriving myself of stuff I loved and cracked on without complaint.

As the months passed by and the seasons changed without word on when a new campaign might start, we fell into a pattern of deferring the VAT, paying the PAYE and managing our dwindling finances. We took the opportunity to carry out much-needed maintenance on and off the pitch. The turf was reseeded, and, without any matches, ended up looking the best it had done for some time. The gents' toilets were fixed and the indoor bar's makeover was completed. I even managed to deal with several practical issues myself, arranging for the fading seats in the Sid Sykes Stand to be replaced so that they proudly displayed the club's initials in vibrant red and white. By June, everything on our checklist had been ticked off – except of course for the TV in the changing rooms.

We all worked as a team, and somehow, by hook or by crook, we made it through the worst. We did what everyone else did, which was our best. Our best for our club, for the community, and most importantly for one another. We tried to be useful and optimistic even when it felt impossible, but mostly we just waited until we could be a football club again.

The Post-match

It's Monday, 11 April 2022, and almost three years since Dad and I took over at the club, the turnstiles of FC United's Broadhurst Park crank into overdrive as just over a thousand bodies pour into the stadium to watch the Frank Hannah Manchester Cup Final. We're set to play our local rivals Hyde United in a match that's been billed as one that could 'save our season'.

Most, if not all, of the club's volunteers, board members and backroom team are sat in the corporate hospitality suite dressed in their Monday-night best. Many are sporting official club-crested blazers or ties that have been dusted off and ironed down after years in hiding. The suite is spacious and smells of fresh paint and fresh food. It's festooned with well-dressed tables adorned with pristine tablecloths. A constantly busy bar boasts bottles of Sauvignon Blanc, beer and Bovril, and the room is kitted out with a state-of-the-art sound system and floor-to-ceiling windows that look out on to an immaculate pitch. It's a beautiful stadium, reportedly built for £6.5 million, and is the envy of the north-western non-league world.

Dad and I are both lost in thought. We sit across from each other nervously picking at our bread rolls in anticipation of a game that will define our tenure at the club so far. The sensation of anxiety mixed with dread and excitement feels reminiscent of waiting for exam results. We're fast approaching an important milestone as chairmen. After three years at the club we are at last only four games away from completing a season.

We've spent the last two years locked in limbo, desperately working to keep the club afloat. After the null-and-voiding of our first season in March 2020 we found our second stop-start season was indefinitely stopped too, this time before we even got to Christmas.

On reflection it was a season that should never have been attempted. Constant Covid outbreaks often saw games postponed or teams being forced to play without half of their players. It was a campaign characterized by sporadic lockdowns and governmental restrictions. The only positive was that, thanks to our low match-day attendances, supporters at Hurst Cross had been practising social distancing since the late 1980s.

We spent most of the time in the bottom half of the table and even more of it without any defenders. Regrettably, most of our back line were schoolteachers, which meant they were almost always forced to isolate. We were nineteenth with just five points on the board when the season was curtailed. Lowlights included a 4–0 hammering by South Shields, a 3–0 mauling at home to Mickleover and a bad-tempered 1–0 defeat at Cleggy's old club Atherton Collieries.

The council also re-closed the outdoor bar, reigniting Dad's one-man battle with the local authorities. The issue this time was that bars without table service were forbidden due to Covid tier-three rules. Thankfully, despite Dad's intentions to take on central government, he saw sense before balancing a fully functioning restaurant (complete with waiters) on top of the terraces just to prove a point.

The only thing worth remembering was getting to the third round proper of the FA Trophy where we were only twenty minutes away from reaching the last sixteen against Kettering. It was an incredible run that saw us graduate from qualifiers to giant-killers after beating the mighty York City on penalties.

At a time of real difficulty those fixtures became a beacon of hope for everyone in the town. Unfortunately, few were able to witness this achievement as most of the matches were played behind closed doors.

After our cup defeat the season was over and the longest pre-season in the history of the sport began. Weeks became months, and the months weren't too far away from a year. We receded into a precarious world of not knowing, of pre-planning for a season that seemed destined never to begin – until, of course, suddenly it did.

Just as quickly as it had stopped, football was back, and this time it was back for good. The turnstiles rolled into life once more as fans and supporters all over the UK were re-united with their long-lost love. The floodlights flickered and the smell of pies, greasy burgers and chips paddling in gravy once again filled the summer air. Hurst Cross was booming (or as close to booming as you can get with a few hundred fans in a 4,000-capacity arena), the new bar, now dubbed the Cross Bar, was open, and after a flurry of new signings we were ready. The Friday-night nerves were back, the WhatsApp groups fired into life, and the feeling of living for the weekend returned, but this time it was heaven. I vowed to myself to ensure that I never took the club, my role or football for granted ever again. I was even pleased to read the pre-season criticism of @TheAnonymousRobin on the once again active unofficial official fans' forum.

The 2021/22 season started with a bang, a bumper crowd of almost 500 and a 2–0 win to boot. It didn't take long for us to get ahead of ourselves and start dreaming of promotion. Unfortunately it turned out to be a season defined by consistent inconsistency and turbulent bouts of bad form. After winning our first match everything went downhill quicker than a boulder on rollerblades. Bad luck seemed to lurk behind every goalpost and a series of last-minute goals and shocking referee decisions meant we went an incredible twelve matches without winning.

Dormant discontent lay dormant no longer and tensions between Dad, me and indeed everyone at the club resurfaced. There were calls to sack the manager, to sack the board, even to sack us; but just when it looked like all was lost our luck finally changed (on match thirteen) and we beat Nantwich Town 2–1. We followed it up with five consecutive wins, rocketing quickly up the table to safety.

Despite the mini-turnaround the damage had already been done, and although on the form table we were never below the top eight again, we'd lost too much ground to get anywhere near the play-offs. We played some wonderful football at times and against top-half teams we were often sublime. Unfortunately, against teams in the bottom third we were almost always ridiculous. A 4–3 defeat away at rock-bottom Grantham stands out as possibly one of the worst days of my life. The hosts were without a home victory in twenty-three games and we were 3–1 up until eighty-four minutes in, when we decided the best course of action was to pretend to be an under-12s side, gifting the opposition the game. The haunted look of disbelief on our supporters' faces will stay with me to the grave. Post-match there was palpable anger and apparently a changing-room bust-up. I drove home in silence, tears pricking at my eyes, genuinely unsure whether I had the strength to continue.

It was undoubtedly a low moment, but it ended up proving a turning point. The next match we played was away at Avro, a team two leagues below us in the North West Counties Premier, in the semi-final of the Manchester Cup. The game was played on a ludicrously bouncy plastic pitch under torrential rain. They scored early from a well-worked goal and were the better team for ninety minutes. Thankfully for us there were three minutes of injury time, and two goals in the dying seconds from new striker Florian Yonsian and Ben Hardcastle saved our blushes and possibly Mike's job too. After looking like we were sleepwalking to a mid-table finish, we found ourselves in a final and in with a chance of winning the local cup for the first time in thirteen years.

To our surprise, the club coach sold out in record time and so did the next one as hundreds of our supporters booked their tickets for the big match. The feeling of excitement grew with every week and there was a sense of destiny in the air when it was announced the final would be played on 11 April, on what would have been the ninetieth birthday of my grandfather, the club's longest-serving captain.

For once everything was going to plan until, as the final approached, a growing injury crisis left us scrambling to pull a team together. It saw Mike forced into taking several risks, with many of the starting eleven not being 100 per cent fit and two of the substitutes not being fit at all.

We head out of the hospitality suite and take our seats. The crowd sings and cheers, some waving home-made flags with club crests, as drums and bugles sound out into the still light sky. The players emerge and the floodlights, keen to get in on the action, spark to life, adding to an already electric atmosphere.

'Let's get this won,' says Dad, squeezing my hand affectionately.

I smile, and grip him tightly on the shoulder. Here we go again, I think to myself as everyone takes their positions.

The match kicks off, and after only eight seconds we're ahead! Michael Brewster plays a beautiful through ball to Ben Hardcastle who makes no mistake. He slots the ball neatly into the bottom corner, sending our larger than normal support into raptures. Dad and I jump up from our seats in celebration alongside Robbo, Angie, Deano, Dale and the rest of my family. We're all so shocked we don't really know what to do with ourselves. It's the perfect start but there's still the entire match to play.

As the game grows into itself, I allow myself to relax a little. We're dominating. The pitch is immaculate and it's allowing us to play some really nice stuff. We almost get a second and I start to imagine how it might feel to lift a cup. For once the post-match interview conducted in my mind is pleasurable and my interlocutor is kind in their questioning.

Then, with just fifteen minutes on the clock, Brewster stops in his tracks, his already pulled hamstring having pulled again. He tries to run it off but he can barely move and we're pushed into an early substitution. Not long after that lightning strikes twice and Shezza does his calf and is forced to come off too. Worryingly, his replacement Nathan Ntalu has just recovered from an injury himself and isn't really fit. Cleggy and Healdy make a series of complex hand gestures to the lads before sitting back pensively in the dugout. We're barely twenty minutes in and we've had to change two of our personnel and our formation.

Suddenly the game turns on its head. It's so end to end it's like basketball and Hyde are starting to get the better of us. They have a good chance but our keeper Greg Hartley is equal to it and makes an incredible acrobatic double save before we have a shout for a penalty turned down.

At the break there's unwanted time to reflect and for the already rising tension to ratchet up. I head back into the hospitality suite barely speaking, going through various scenarios in my head, ways in which we could throw away our lead. I'm so distracted I don't notice Reginald stealing my complimentary cheese plate from right under my nose. 'Nice Edam,' he says, shaking me from my reverie. Dad stands at the bar with Mum, Angie and Robbo, all of them looking sallow and clammy. My wife Lucy looks up from her book and asks me the score. I can't tell if she's joking.

The second half gets underway, and Dad and I are no longer

able to sit down. Every sound from the crowd makes me more and more nervous. We banish ourselves to the back of the main stand and watch on our feet, pacing frantically between the two sets of commentators who're sat at little desks reporting on the game.

The noise of the crowd is spectacular. There aren't just a few stragglers singing and shouting, everyone in attendance is doing their bit to make this a special night. The Ashton supporters, marshalled by Stella, are in full voice but the Hyde fans are equal to the challenge. They roar their team forward as slowly the momentum of the match starts to swing.

We look tired. There are players on the pitch who haven't played for months and gaps are starting to open up all over the place. Hyde blast the ball narrowly wide before our central defender Harry Coates saves the day, sliding across the box to block a certain goal.

They pile on the pressure, having chance after chance as we start to give away cheap free kicks like gifts at Christmas. It feels like only a matter of time before they draw level. Cleggy waves his arms furiously, trying to spark a third wind in the legs of our leggy side. It's not doing much good though, and on seventy-six minutes a long ball from deep isn't dealt with and their forward blasts it into the top corner.

Half of the stadium erupts and I literally fall to my knees, crumpled in a heap. The best chance we have now is penalties and even then it's going to be tough to hang on. As I bury my head in my hands I hear a cheer from our supporters. We've been granted a reprieve! I'm not sure if it's offside or a foul on our defender but the flag is up and the goal has been disallowed. The colour returns to Dad's face and I shriek with pleasure as if we've just scored another goal.

The clock continues to count down and my heart starts pounding. I'd most likely mug an elderly relative if it guaranteed the win. I've lost the plot. I scream and complain at everything, my body suddenly full of more testosterone than at any time throughout my puberty. There are over ten minutes left to play and still more twists in the tale to come.

When the electronic scoreboard is raised there are also a mammoth eight minutes of stoppage time to endure. I bite down on my knuckles and start to pray to every god I can think of. Nathan Ntalu has run himself into the ground since he came on and receives a huge round of applause as currently injured centre-half Sam Baird is brought on in his stead to help shore up the defence.

Hyde go for broke. They launch the ball forward but we defend heroically. The end is so near but it feels further away than when we started. Time grinds to a halt and each minute starts to feel like a lifetime. Our supporters whistle and gesture at their wrists, pointing to invisible watches in the hope that it might push the referee into ending the game early.

With seconds left on the clock, Hyde's winger intercepts the ball and breaks down the right-hand side of the pitch, whipping in a tantalizing cross. I watch through my fingers as Dad turns away in nervous despair. It's headed on to the post and ricochets back, smacking our goalkeeper right in the face. All hell breaks loose as the ball bounces around the box like a ping-pong ball on espresso before Greg finally grabs it and falls gratefully to the ground.

The ball is cleared and the referee blows his whistle.

We've done it! Cheers ring out across the stadium. I holler in defiance as Dad rushes over to me.

'Get in!' we scream at each other.

'I love you!' I shout.

'I love you too!' he screams back, red-faced with delight.

Robbo and Angie rush over. They're literally jumping at us with joy. We dance around like lunatics and we're soon joined by our commentary team, my mum, my sister, my wife Lucy and the rest of my family. I fist-bump strangers and hug two old stern-faced men in FA blazers. 'We've won a cup! We've won a cup!' I shout at them as I head to the edge of the stand and look over on to the pitch and at our supporters.

It's one of the loveliest moments I can remember. Tom and Bethany are wearing AUFC bobble hats on their heads and grins on their faces. Phil and his partner (still wearing the same fleece) share an awkward embrace while Bryan and his husband Ash sigh with collective relief. Mavis screams at her grandson Pete who smiles and wraps her under his arm. I spot Larry, now a little frailer but still full of life. He waves his stick enthusiastically, with our long-standing president Reginald and frequent protester Frank Taunton stood either side of him applauding energetically. Tony Liverstout nods in approval as kids in Little Robins tracksuits wave happily, underscored by the marching beat of Stella's drum. By the seats near the tunnel, two men sing boisterously while another dabs his teary eyes. It's Neville Peterson, aka @TheAnonymousRobin. I check my phone – he's posting live on Facebook: 'WHAT A NIGHT!' On the pitch the players hug, congratulating one another on a job well done, as Deano and Dale, joined by Georgina and his son Simon, dart around with glee. It means so much to see them briefly enjoy some fruit from their endless labour.

'What are you doing up there, gents?' Mike shouts up towards Dad and me. 'This is your cup too!'

It's all a bit of a blur from there. We run down on to the pitch, a sea of high fives and congratulations flooding our senses. It's everything I'd dreamed of when we came to the club. We're cajoled on to the grass and instantly we're in the thick of it. We're chest-bumping and clutching the squad in thanks and I'm lifted into the air and passed around like a floppy parcel as the entire AUFC family celebrate en masse. The cup is brought out by a series of officials and our supporters begin to serenade the team with a rendition of '*Campioni! Campioni! Olé, olé, olé!*'

'Here you go, boys,' shouts Mike, handing us the trophy.

Dad and I grip a handle each and run towards the crowd. They cheer as we hold our arms aloft. After so many defeats and disappointments we are, at least for now, victorious. I look around and see the blissful faces that surround me and feel utter contentment. The voice in my head telling me I'm useless is silent and the imposter syndrome that has overwhelmed my time at the club has evaporated. I'm just totally in the moment – and in this moment Dad, myself and everyone at the club are just happy.

If this was a Hollywood movie then this is where the story would end: father and son, delighting in their triumph, surrounded by their team, their manager and the friends they've made along the way. After moments of division and anger they now stand together, united by the trophy that they hold up to the heavens, their grandfather and father no doubt looking down on them with pride. The supporters continue to cheer and sing their names as the screen fades to black and the credits roll.

Unfortunately this was not a movie and the story certainly didn't end there. Shortly after this moment a bottle of fizz was popped and as players and staff celebrated I ran behind them all and, unseen by everyone except one bewildered FA official, I vomited all over the pitch and my shoes. Dad and I would later that very evening have a drunken argument about whether the opening goal was scored inside the first minute or not, and one of our supporters would drop the trophy on the floor, breaking it beyond repair. We would also lose all of our final three league matches, 2–0, 3–0 and 5–0, finishing fourteenth, clear of trouble but miles off the play-offs.

I've long since realized that the idea of everything 'clicking into place' is a fantasy and that in football you need to learn to live from week to week and match to match. It's a game of emotion that extends beyond being just a sport. It's a global phenomenon that keeps everyone stuck on a see-saw, relentlessly rocking between eternal hope and infinite despair. It's stressful and gut-wrenching but also capable of delivering a joy so powerful that it can transcend anything. It's why we all love it. It's why no matter how devastating the loss, no matter how bruising the experience, we always come back for more.

As Tony said on our very first day at his office, 'it's a roller-coaster', full of ups and downs and never short of surprises. I've learnt that the real winners of the game are those who can learn to enjoy the ride, be grateful for the experience and be able to take the rough with the smooth in equal measure, or, as that guy who sold all those fruit pies once said, to treat triumph and disaster in the same way. I'm determined to be one of those people going forward.

I'm writing this sat at the desk in my office, the 2022/23 season now just over the halfway point. It's been a mixed start for us – we're thirteenth, nine points from the play-offs, and sailing has been anything but smooth.

We've once again been deducted points for fielding an ineligible player (despite that player having played for us for three seasons). We've had a virulent strain of flu spread through the squad, robbing us of half our starting line-up, and our women's team have had to downgrade for the season to a seven-a-side team due to a lack of numbers. We've had the usual last-minute wins and defeats and the budget has once again gotten away from us. Dad and I have been at each other's throat but also by each other's side.

After two heavy defeats against local rivals and a decline in results and playing style, manager Michael Clegg stepped down from his role and another new era began. Jamie Cunningham arrived and with him a raft of players full of talent and promise and a bullish mentality. His tenure got off to a fabulous start with a 3–0 win against Warrington Rylands but a cold snap stopped any momentum before it could start as games across the country were cancelled due to hard frost. There is, however, a growing feeling that this time things might be different.

Off the field the club enjoyed its fifteen minutes of fame

when a tweet saying we were trying to sign Erling Haaland captured not just the country's attention but the world's. Club officials and staff were interviewed on TV and radio stations from north-west England to Australia, and even made it on to Sky Sports News. The tweet was eventually seen by over 40 million people and Ashton United briefly became part of mainstream football's vernacular. Calls to increase our media manager Matt's wages were heard and as a volunteer his salary of £0K per annum was doubled on the spot.

Despite the global coverage, we still struggled to sell enough tickets to break even on our New Year's Eve party. We launched a new beer named by our supporters after our captain. The Special Brewster was a roaring success, selling at unprecedented speed until Brewster was moved on by our new manager to Radcliffe Borough, leaving us with an armband to fill and a stock cupboard full of novelty booze to empty.

I have no idea if we'll be able to make it into the top five this season, or indeed if we'll even get back into the promised land of the National League North. Promotion is still a pipe dream and I'm not sure if we'll be able to deliver on many, or even any, of the promises we made to our supporters all that time ago.

The only thing I do know is this: non-league football is bad for your health but good for the soul. It's full of remarkable people doing remarkable things, working themselves to the bone for the love of the game and their community. My life has no doubt been shortened by becoming the co-chairman of Ashton United but it's also been hugely enriched. I've met some of the most generous and caring people I'll ever meet and I've made friendships that will last a lifetime. I've been able to connect with my local community and find a sense of belonging that's hard to come by.

Working with my dad has been simultaneously a dream come true and a living nightmare. Nearly four years into the job there's still nowhere to hide, nowhere to run. It's not always easy and I'm sure there'll be many more bumps in the road. But I can say with my hand on my heart that there's nowhere I'd rather be and there's nobody I'd rather be doing this with.

Acknowledgements

Lucy Danser, David Burke, Janet Burke, Lucy Burke, David Luxton, Henry Vines, Nicki Stoddart, Thomas Hill, Jamie Hobson, Jackie Tierney, Andrew Finnigan, Carol Finnigan, Patrick Finnigan, Andy Clayton, Matt Clayton, Dave Nolan, Pete Barrett, Pete O'Brien, Michael Anderson, John Milne, Andy Evans, Mick Cummings, Ronnie Thomason, Michael Bennet, Kevin Wickham, Jeremy Sayle, Dave Robinson, Wayne Schofield, Luke Sayle, Brian Kay, Brian Marshal, Catherine Tomlinson, Chris Tomlinson, Vic Tomlinson, Nigel Keogh, Ryan Smith, Tony Williams and Sian Binks. Jake Emery, Tom Langford, Tom Grose, Michael Clegg, Andy Heald, Jody Banim, Simon Woodford, Kieran Bently, Damian Crossely, Nicky Hunt, James Eachus, Liam Welsby, Mel Pemberton, Karen Greene, Trish Bromley, Michael Brewster, Sam Sheridan, Greg Hartley, Ben Hardcastle, Demi Graham, Jamie Cunningham and all the wonderful volunteers and supporters at Ashton United.

Up the Robins!

About the Author

Jonathan Sayer is an award-winning comedy playwright and screenwriter. He is the co-author of *The Play That Goes Wrong* (with Henry Lewis and Henry Shields), *Peter Pan Goes Wrong*, *The Comedy About a Bank Robbery*, *Groan Ups*, *Magic Goes Wrong* (with Penn & Teller), *The Mind Mangler Member of The Tragic Circle* and *The Goes Wrong Show* (BBC One – series 1 and 2). He is a writer, performer and creative director of Mischief Comedy. His work has been performed internationally in forty-nine territories, including the West End and Broadway.

As a footballer, Jonathan played his only competitive game for AFC Stanley Tigers U13s in the late nineties. He was brought on as a half-time substitute and substituted again shortly after gifting the opposition three goals in five minutes. After his debut, Accrington Stanley ended its official ties to the team and Jonathan took the decision to hang up his brand-new boots for good.